"This book is a wonderful enc̶ [...] ten
men described are African-Ai [...] not
matter nearly as much as thei [...] are
sufficiently diverse that they [...] gh
similarity that together they l [...] of
his Son. Read this book and r̶ [...]

...n Professor of New Testament,
Trinity Evangelical Divinity School

"Here we have readable, compelling personal histories that, at the same time, teach us more about God, Christ, and the Bible and give accounts of these men coming to Christ. I love reading people's testimonies of conversion! What more do we want in a book? To be encouraged, instructed, and edified, read these stories."

Mark Dever, Senior Pastor, Capitol Hill Baptist Church, Washington, DC

"A reading of *Glory Road* is a journey of sober rejoicing. The joy is in the taste of future glory where men and women from every tribe and language and people and nation will together worship the Lamb. We rejoice in the first fruits of that glory evident in the testimonies of these gifted African-Americans now in Reformed churches. We also weep that their testimonies are so few due to these churches' long blindness to gospel priorities despite their historic commitment to doctrinal orthodoxy. May *Glory Road* lead to a new dawn, greeted with tears but leading to songs of joy before the day is done."

Bryan Chapell, President, Covenant Theological Seminary

"I'm very grateful for Anthony Carter's passion for writing. I bought a case of his first book— *On Being Black and Reformed*, to distribute at conferences and events. My plan is to do the same thing with *Glory Road*, an amazing collection of testimonies. The consistent message from all the contributors is the paucity of Reformed teaching in the black community. I share with Carl Ellis the vision of seeing an indigenous Reformed movement in the African-American community. Books like *Glory Road* will help to facilitate this movement."

Wy Plummer, African-American Ministries Coordinator,
Mission to North America, Presbyterian Church in America

"History is good for us all, but when you see it occurring right before your eyes, well that's just about as good as it gets. To the chorus of 'Dead White Men,' we now add these voices of Living Color. Together we'll all be singing praises to our sovereign God and all-sufficient Savior."

Stephen J. Nichols, Research Professor of Christianity and Culture,
Lancaster Bible College

"As a first-generation preacher of Reformed Theology in Antigua and Barbuda and the eastern Caribbean, I am confident and encouraged that these personal testimonies from our African-American brothers will work for a wider propagation of the message of the supremacy of God in all things throughout the global African Diaspora. The common themes of being disillusioned with the religious status quo, struggling with the inadequacy of man-centered views that were strongly defended for years, facing the loneliness and ostracism of taking a stand on an island of truth in a sea of pluralism, and the surprising discovery that the Lord had all along 'reserved . . . seven thousand men, who have not bowed the knee to the image of Baal,' are all compelling and refreshing in the narrative of each experience."

Hensworth W. C. Jonas, Executive Director,
East Caribbean Baptist Mission, St. John's, Antigua & Barbuda

"Glory to God for the things he has done! I too join in the celebration of the lives of these wonderful men. Their journeys of faith speak to God's redemption, power, providence, and sovereignty. As I read through this book, I reflected on my own life which includes spending twelve years as a Pentecostal pastor and then entering Covenant Seminary in 1992. I never gave Calvinism too much thought before then, but God had a marvelous plan for me. I really appreciate Reformed theology and the impact that it is having on the African American PCA congregation that I serve today. God bless you Brother Carter for your vision to create this precious book. Lord, send us more black leadership!"

Mike Higgins, Senior Pastor,
Redemption Fellowship Presbyterian Church in America, Atlanta

Also edited by Anthony J. Carter:

Experiencing the Truth:
Bringing the Reformation to the African-American Church

Glory Road

The Journeys of
10 African-Americans
into Reformed Christianity

Edited by Anthony J. Carter

CROSSWAY BOOKS
WHEATON, ILLINOIS

Glory Road: The Journeys of 10 African-Americans into Reformed Christianity
Copyright © 2009 by Anthony J. Carter

Published by Crossway Books
    a publishing ministry of Good News Publishers
    1300 Crescent Street
    Wheaton, Illinois 60187

Cover design: Josh Dennis
Illustrations by: Dave Hopkins
Interior design and typesetting by: Lakeside Design Plus
First printing 2009
Printed in the United States of America

Unless otherwise indicated, Scripture quotations are from the ESV® Bible (*The Holy Bible, English Standard Version*®), copyright © 2001 by Crossway Bibles, a publishing ministry of Good News Publishers. Used by permission. All rights reserved.

Scripture quotations marked KJV are from the *King James Version* of the Bible.

Scripture quotations marked NIV are from *The Holy Bible: New International Version*®. Copyright © 1973, 1978, 1984 by International Bible Society. Used by permission of Zondervan Publishing House. All rights reserved.

    The "NIV" and "New International Version" trademarks are registered in the United States Patent and Trademark Office by International Bible Society. Use of either trademark requires the permission of International Bible Society.

All emphases in Scripture quotations have been added.

Trade Paperback ISBN: 978-1-4335-0584-3
PDF ISBN: 978-1-4335-0585-0
Mobipocket ISBN: 978-1-4335-0586-7

Library of Congress Cataloging-in-Publication Data
Glory road : the journeys of 10 African-Americans into Reformed Christianity / edited by Anthony J. Carter.
      p. cm.
    Includes bibliographical references and index.
    ISBN 978-1-4335-0584-3 (tpb)
    1. African American Reformed (Reformed Church)—Biography. 2. Reformed Church converts—United States—Biography. I. Carter, Anthony J., 1967–
II. Title.

BX9498.A37G56 2009
284'.273092396073—dc22
[B]   2008054454

VP		20	19	18	17	16	15	14	13	12	11	10	09
14	13	12	11	10	9	8	7	6	5	4	3	2	1

To R. C. Sproul.
When God inspired 1 Corinthians 15:58,
we believe he had men like you in mind.

Thus says the LORD: "Stand by the roads, and look, and ask for the ancient paths, where the good way is; and walk in it, and find rest for your souls . . ." (Jer. 6:16).

Contents

Contributors

Reddit Andrews III (MDiv, Trinity Evangelical Divinity School) serves as senior pastor of Soaring Oaks Presbyterian Church in Elk Grove, CA.

Thabiti Anyabwile (MS, North Carolina State University) serves as senior pastor of First Baptist Church of Grand Cayman in the Cayman Islands.

Anthony B. Bradley (PhD, Westminster Theological Seminary) serves as Assistant Professor of Systematic Theology and Ethics at Covenant Theological Seminary in St. Louis and Research Fellow for the Acton Institute for the Study of Religion and Liberty in Grand Rapids, MI.

Anthony J. Carter (MA, Reformed Theological Seminary) serves as lead pastor of East Point Church in East Point, GA.

Ken Jones (BS, Pepperdine University) serves as senior pastor of Greater Union Baptist Church in Compton, CA, and is cohost of the nationally syndicated radio program *The White Horse Inn*.

Michael Leach (MA, Reformed Theological Seminary) serves as pastor of All Saints Redeemer Church in Stone Mountain, GA, and teaches theology and homiletics at American University of Biblical Studies in Decatur, GA.

Lance Lewis (MA, Chesapeake Theological Seminary) serves as pastor of Christ Liberation Fellowship in Philadelphia.

Louis C. Love Jr. serves as pastor of New Life Fellowship Church in Vernon Hills, IL.

Eric C. Redmond (ThM, Dallas Theological Seminary) serves as Assistant Professor of Bible and Theology at Washington Bible College in Lanham, MD.

Roger Skepple (ThM, Dallas Theological Seminary) serves as senior pastor of Berean Bible Baptist Church in Atlanta.

Preface

This is a book about ordinary men who have been brought to believe and preach an extraordinary God who has wrought an extraordinary salvation in their lives. Without a doubt this has been the most encouraging and rewarding project I have had the privilege of working on. I consider the men in this volume to be friends, colleagues, and brothers-in-arms in the battle of ideas. Writing, reading, and editing this book has been a joy.

When I first got the idea for this book, these were the first men that came to mind. All responded with enthusiasm and gratefulness. Indeed, the eager response I had anticipated was one of the reasons why I approached them. I knew they had hearts for biblical theology and its promotion among the people of God. I knew further that they had hearts for proclaiming Reformed theology where it has not been faithfully and fruitfully proclaimed, namely among African-Americans. I knew this because I have held hands with each of these brothers on various occasions and have had the distinct pleasure of hearing and learning of their hearts. Indeed it is from the heart that this book proceeds, and we pray that it is to your heart that this book would go.

After receiving the support of the authors of this volume, I needed to find a publisher that would be enthusiastic and unapologetic in its excitement for this project. It did not take long. At the top of our list was Crossway Books. It was the first to receive our proposal and the first to respond. The response was immediate and sincere; we could not have asked for more. Thus, I would like to give my grateful and enthusiastic thanks to Allan Fisher, Jill Carter, and Tara Davis, and all the good people at Crossway Books. Their commitment to publishing sound, biblical material is an encouragement to the entire body of Christ.

We are aware that we stand in a line of faithful men who have affirmed and continue to affirm the glorious theology we graciously hold. While we have dedicated this book to R. C. Sproul because he has played such a key role in our development, we understand that he is not alone. There have been faithful contemporary African-American men who have long held to Reformation truth and have preached it for years. Men like Dr. Robert J. Cameron, Carl Ellis, Wy Plummer, and others have paved the way and continue to pave the way for another generation of Reformed-minded African-American thinkers and preachers. Though they were not included in this volume, their lives and ministries deserve books of their own. We are indebted to God for their labors and give God thanks for them. Furthermore, it is fitting that this book should be published in the year of John Calvin's five hundredth birthday. As the church remembers the undeniable impact of Calvin's teaching and life, we are glad to consider ourselves the grateful beneficiaries of the Christ-centered, biblically-grounded theology he labored so diligently to teach and preach.

In this volume you will read of men who made mistakes and frequently assumed God's will without careful consideration. Consequently, you will wonder what our wives were thinking, and how they managed to endure the ever-changing frustrations of our journeys. Time and space does not allow for a detailed account of the faithfulness of our wives (that is perhaps another book in itself). But for the record, we give thanks to God for his gifts of grace, our wives. God has used them to keep our fuels mixed and the engines running on our journeys. It is because of them that we are in positions to soberly and joyfully recount our journeys into the truths we hold so dear. We thank God that he has worked in our wives' lives so that they hold these truths to be dear as well.

Finally, although the name of this book is *Glory Road: The Journeys of 10 African-Americans into Reformed Christianity*, neither the glory nor the road is ours. They belong to God and God alone. While he does not share his glory, he does invite all to share the road. We pray that when reading our stories, you will get a glimpse of God's glory and would be moved to come and share the road.

Anthony J. Carter

Introduction

KEN JONES

A number of years ago General Motors launched an ad campaign for its line of Buick automobiles in an effort to dispel the notion that Buicks were more suited for senior citizens. The slogan adopted for this campaign was "This Is Not Your Father's Oldsmobile." In many respects American Protestants are doing the same thing with historic Protestantism. It is as if we take great pride that this is not the Protestantism of Martin Luther, John Calvin, George Whitefield, Jonathan Edwards, and others. This is not the Protestantism of the historic confessions and catechisms. In short, only a fraction of the millions of professing evangelical Christians in America would identify themselves as Reformed, reformational, intentionally Calvinistic, or by whatever label that could be attached to those who embrace the theology of our Protestant forefathers. This volume, however, is not just about contemporary Christians who are not ashamed to embrace reformational Christianity. The contributors to this volume are African-American churchmen who openly adhere to historic Protestantism and the doctrines of grace. If it is rare for an American Christian in general to hold such convictions today, it is twice as rare for an African-American Christian. For the contributors to this present work, the doctrines they embrace and expound are truly "not their father's doctrines."

When one thinks of an African-American Christian, a number of things might come to mind: a Baptist (freewill, of course), a Methodist, a Pentecostal, a quasi-Pentecostal, or even perhaps an adherent to the Prosperity Gospel or the Social Gospel. What one does not routinely expect to encounter is an African-American Christian who consciously embraces the theology of Luther, Calvin, and Edwards. These contributors don't just enjoy reading these theologians of the past, and they do not simply glean their writings for good preaching material. No, they have plumbed the depths of systematic and biblical theology and have come out on the side of those who stand under the banner of Reformed or reformational theology. They have consciously rejected the anthropology of Pelagius, the soteriology of Wesley, the pneumatology of Azusa Street, the methodology of Finney, and similar systems of religious thought and expression.

So what do we mean by Reformed theology or the doctrines of grace? It is almost impossible to do justice to this broad theological subject in just a few short paragraphs. But I will try.

The most common summation of Reformed theology is the five points of Calvinism, couched in the acrostic TULIP: T=Total depravity, U=Unconditional election, L=Limited atonement, I=Irresistible grace, and P=Perseverance of the saints. What permeates these five points is the sovereignty and glory of God in our salvation. It begins with man's total depravity, a result of the fall, which renders him utterly incapable of responding to the gospel, and ends with God persevering with his people to the end in spite of endless temptations and failures that face them. At the end of the day all glory is directed to the sovereign God who saves. It is his plan of salvation that is efficacious.

Reformed theology is also covenantal; God's plan of salvation as revealed in Scripture is presented in a covenantal framework. Covenant is not superimposed on the Scripture as some may charge, but is interwoven throughout its narrative. Reformed theology unwraps the covenant language of Scripture, bringing to light important concepts and terms such as covenant of works, covenant of grace, covenant mediator, federal head, and signs and seals.

Finally, Reformed theology is christocentric. All of God's saving works are accomplished in and by his only begotten Son. Jesus did not just die for our sins; in his life he performed the righteousness that God requires of us. Christ is the theme of all of Scripture. He is the prophet that proclaims the Word of God to his people for salvation (gospel) and to the world for judgment (law). All prophets that came before Christ prefigured and pointed to his unique prophetic office. And every faithful preacher since his coming declares his Word and stands in his authority.

Christ is our High Priest who has offered the one acceptable sacrifice for human sin. All other priests and their sacrifices pointed to Christ, and it is the promise of his coming that gave them significance, but Christ is the substance. Christ is our King who conquers our enemies, provides for our needs, and governs us through his Word. Reformed theology stresses union with Christ because in him are all the riches of God's grace. Without union with him we are still in our sins and under the condemnation of a just and holy God. Reformed theology is offensive to other doctrinal systems because it lays the ax to the root of human works and ability as the means of being justified before God.

The question this volume seeks to answer is, how? How did these men come to their theological and doctrinal understanding and conviction? But as the question of "how?" is addressed, the greater question arises—why? Why have these men chosen to part ways with the religious traditions and system that served as a catalyst for the Civil Rights Movement? On the surface it would appear that these African-American churchmen have sided with a system of religion that provided theological support for the oppression of our forefathers, and that they stand in opposition to traditional African-American Christianity that has been hailed as the impetus for our liberation. Of course, that view is shortsighted, superficial, and simplistic to say the least. But it still leads to the question of, why? The answer that permeates each chapter is the conviction from the Word of God. These men have reached a point in their Christian walks where they are convinced that Christianity as articulated by the Protestant Reformation is the Christianity of the Bible. Though surrounded by inconsistent application and gross misrepresentation of the doctrines of grace, these writers have chosen to stand in the rich biblical and systematic theology of men with whom there are significant differences and disagreements on very important social and ethical issues. In some cases taking that stand has caused others to label them "pariah" or "sell-out" along with other derogatory and denigrating remarks. But nonetheless they remain undaunted in their conviction that the gospel is properly understood only through the doctrines of grace. This has emboldened them to take the road less traveled, so to speak.

This bold stance has led some of them to step outside the bounds of denominations traditionally associated with African-American Christians and join historically Reformed denominations such as the Presbyterian Church in America (PCA). Some have remained within their denominations, but have committed to a different message and a different vision of the church from what they previously held. Still others have decided not to be denominationally affiliated and seek to pave new avenues for Reformed theology among African-American Christians.

Having considered the unique challenges inherent in bringing reformational theology to the context of the African-American church, I must hasten to add that this book is not just "a black thing" with no relevance or bearing outside the black church. As I stated before, the doctrines of grace are noticeably absent in most American evangelical churches. Therefore the essays in this volume can be helpful for any Christian or preacher who has recognized that something is drastically missing in American evangelicalism. It is my prayer that in reading this volume, those who have taken on the challenge of "reforming" a church will be greatly encouraged and assisted in their work. And may others be challenged to discover the more excellent foundation of the doctrines of grace and join us on the journey along the glory road.

1

A Plea for Real Answers

REDDIT ANDREWS III

I come from a long line of Baptist preachers and deacons. From my earliest memories growing up in Hartford, Connecticut, I was not only conscious of God, but intensely interested in spiritual things. I have vivid memories of maintaining a constant inner dialogue with God. I remember getting dressed on Sunday mornings when I was around seven, putting on my little clip-on necktie, and consciously trying to set my face and mimic the walk of the deacons at Mount Calvary Baptist Church where I attended and my grandfather served as deacon. My most precious memories include the look on his face when he assisted in my baptism one evening service when I was seven or eight years old.

As wonderful as those memories are, they are not totally unclouded. Those silver clouds were laced with dark strains of doubts I never spoke of. I will never know what sort of help I might have received, because I simply suppressed them. I recall getting a McDonald's map of the solar system and taping it to the wall next to my pillow. I'd sometimes spend moments that seemed like hours gazing at it, impressed by the vastness of space.

This would give rise to troubling thoughts. *How could a God so great and powerful as to make all that exists in outer space possibly know me? Is it conceivable that he can really hear my prayers? Even if it were possible, would he even care?* To my young mind these thoughts were deep and unsettling.

My inner struggles were compounded by the powerful conflicting messages I was exposed to in public school. It was not difficult for me to see that the message I was receiving in school and the message I was receiving in my Sunday school classes were mutually exclusive. In public school, my Sunday morning lessons were flatly contradicted. I dutifully listened in Sunday school where I was taught how God created the world in the space of six days and how he rested on the seventh. All week long I would lug around school books that said the earth was millions of years old and that mankind evolved over an unfathomably lengthy period of time. As a child it seemed quite easy to decide who was correct. My Sunday school teachers were mainly the parents of friends, housewives, and bus drivers. The church was an old unimpressive structure, while to my young mind, the school I attended was a large, impressive, building. My teachers appeared highly trained and incredibly competent. Furthermore, there were so many books, movies, and scaled models at which I could look and even touch.

While I never thought my Sunday school teachers were bad, I just concluded that the public school teachers couldn't possibly be wrong. No, my Sunday school teachers were certainly good people, just misguided and behind the times. Having concluded that, I continued to attend Sunday services for a while, until I became interested in football and girls.[1] My family later moved into a neighborhood where I knew very few people. The kids there seemed louder, more boisterous and violent than what I was accustomed to. I sought comfort in a small Lutheran church in the community. I'd at times gaze out the window while the mostly Anglo and female Sunday school teachers would teach us songs about Jesus. "Lowly Jesus meek and mild, he wouldn't hurt a little child." There was a basketball court on the church property, and I'd watch the games while the lesson was being taught. I would overhear the arguments about the games and watch the fights that would often break out. I'd think to myself, *Man, Jesus needs to hurt some of these children!* My Sunday school experiences all seemed so hopelessly irrelevant and out of touch with real life.

Going My Own Way

I concluded after one of the more tepid classes that though Jesus was plenty nice, he didn't understand my world, and I'd just have to go out and make a name for myself. After all, I reasoned, I was the oldest child in a single parent home; if I didn't, it would be only a matter of time before my home would be disrespected and my little brothers bullied. It was then that I consciously turned my back on God and his church and set about becoming self-sufficient, quietly instilling self-confidence in my siblings. I'd preach fiery messages to them about standing up for themselves, sticking together, and letting no one, ever, under any circumstances disrespect them! Obviously this marked a radical shift in the direction of my life. In fact, it marked the beginning of an odyssey of sin, pain, and shame that engulfed the next fifteen years. It wasn't that those years contained no good, but the sin and rebellion I brought into my heart infiltrated and infected everything I touched. Those years can be aptly summarized by an illustration I heard somewhere: "Knock, knock." "Who's there?" said the man within. "One little sin," was the reply. "Slip in," said the man. All hell walked in.

As I recount my past determination to live without God, three things strike me. First, how swift and complete the fall was! I took to my new life of sin with astonishing ease. Earlier in my life I had worked out some principles for myself, a sort of internal list of things I wouldn't do. It didn't take long for me to blast right through the list, rationalizing each new level of depravity I had sunk to. Second, I'm still shocked at the deception I practiced on myself. I somehow was able to convince myself that I had incredible self-discipline and that eventually I'd grow tired of the life I was living, galvanize my will, and reverse the course I was on. Third, how persistently my conscience plagued me! A battle raged within me, which I was careful to let no one ever suspect I was fighting. Try as I might to get God out of my mind, it wasn't as easy to walk away from him as I had supposed. He was terribly tenacious. I had periods when I thought I'd vanquished him from my heart and mind, only to have him return. He'd wake me at night and haunt me during the days.

Over the years God sent messengers to me and graciously mitigated the consequences of my mulish rebellion. The simple message that Christ came into the world to save sinners and that he died on the cross as a substitute for those he would bring to himself through faith just seemed childish. The thought that someone dying two thousand years earlier could somehow matter to me seemed so utterly foolish and preposterous—I could believe almost anything but that. Yet, nothing else gave me any solace from the gnawing uncertainty I felt within.

In December 1981 I met Nadine, who later became my wife and the mother of my two daughters, Felice and Shannon. Nadine, though unconverted at the time, was raised in the church and attended youth group meetings into her teens. Somehow meeting her created a desire to get serious about turning my life around. Reality came crashing in on me. I'd comforted myself that when I was ready, I'd be able to summon a secret reserve of willpower from within and muscle up moral rectitude. It was devastating to realize that I was unable to overcome the least negative habit I'd fallen into.[2] I discovered the reality of what the Bible calls the dominion of sin. My sins seemed to be interconnected and mutually supportive of one another, continually cooperating to prevent me from ever escaping. I was trapped, helpless, and completely powerless to move toward God. What was worse, the harder I tried, the worse I seemed to grow; I secretly became filled with despair.

A New Year, a New Life

It was December 31, 1987, when the Lord mercifully delivered me. What happened to me that New Year's Eve was nothing short of miraculous! God changed my heart! I had been drinking and was lying awake somewhat giving attention to the televised countdown at Times Square. Almost imperceptibly my thoughts turned to God. I was shocked fully awake by the sudden awareness that I was contemplating him with full knowledge that he not only existed but was cognizant of me—that he knew my thoughts, my sin. I began to think of what justification I could offer for what my life had become. I'd no sooner formulate an excuse than I'd dismiss it as worthless. There was no excuse I could use that would fool God. My thoughts then turned to the terror of hell and the awful eternal separation from all that is good and lovely in life. In terror I thought of all the messengers I had rejected over the years and how I had mistreated them.

I suddenly knew it was true—Christ really had died, and God really would forgive me on the basis of what Jesus had done. That formerly foolish message suddenly was the most glorious thing I had ever heard.[3] I could not see how I had ever doubted it. What was more wondrous was that he seemed to shatter the bars of sin that confined me. A new power and ability suddenly appeared and began to grow within me.

It was as if I had been rescued from a long stint in a dungeon. I staggered out into the marvelous newfound light of God's love. It was as if I had been given a brand-new pair of eyes. The sky seemed brighter, the grass appeared greener, and a freedom came into my heart that had not come from the world but from heaven. Oh, the joy the forgiveness of sin and fellowship with God brought into my life! I was controlled by a desire to tell everyone I could, to find God's people and associate myself with them. I immediately began reading the Bible with a thirst and satisfaction I had never experienced before. The dialogue I had with God as a child resumed, but it became sweeter than anything I had ever imagined and more real than the very air I breathed. Within a week I began attending services at First Baptist Church in Hartford. Very early on I felt in my heart that God wanted me to serve him in the full-time pastoral ministry. But I sensed this wasn't something one should rush into, so I hid this desire in my heart and was content to wait on God's timing.

J. I. Packer once said that God is incredibly tender with his newborns. This was definitely true of my experience. However, the time soon came for me to grow in ways reminiscent of my childhood. Nagging questions and doubts slowly but certainly began to emerge. Little did I suspect that God was purposefully leading me along a path he ordained before the foundation of the world.[4]

Although I could not articulate it at the time, I craved the very same thing I had craved as a child but had been afraid to ask for: I was hungry for a theological foundation for my faith. God, in his goodness, gave me a mind that was logical and craved consistency. I desperately wanted solid reasons behind my faith in God; I was unwilling to completely embrace the gospel if it meant I had to check my brain at the door.[5] Unfortunately, the problem my church had fallen into, and too many churches suffer from today, is that it had discarded historic Christian theology.[6] For some time I thought it was a malady that was unique to the African-American church, but I have since discovered the problem to be more broadly shared than I had originally imagined. This departure manifested itself in several ways that caused me great spiritual difficulty.

Discarding Historic Theology

First, by turning away from historic theology, the church uncritically embraced many other theologies that were not only egregious departures from the teaching of the Bible but were often mutually contradictory. This often resulted in contradictory interpretations of the same passages of Scripture. I would listen to a message, intending to put it into practice in my life, only to have it reversed from the very same pulpit a short time later. I grew confused, frustrated, and then jaded. Chief among the aberrant theological headwinds that ripped through African-American churches was the Prosperity Gospel—the teaching that God wanted everyone to be rich, and by the right exercise of faith we could change our financial condition. I saw this as flying in the face of the Scriptures. I read in the Bible that we should be content with what God has provided, and that failing to do so implies that God is a bad parent (Matt. 6:32; 1 Tim. 6:8). The Bible seemed to teach plainly that the normal Christian life involved difficulty, suffering, and persecution. But this prosperity teaching brazenly contradicted Paul's brave words to the saints at Lystra, Iconium, and Antioch: "through many tribulations we must enter the kingdom of God" (Acts 14:22). Elsewhere the Bible held up men who suffered obvious deprivation as godly and worth emulating (1 Cor. 4:11; Heb. 11:37), but I was being told that financial lack was a sign of my unbelief. I watched as biblical passage after biblical passage was systematically twisted to reflect this monstrous teaching. I saw many individuals encounter significant difficulties as they embraced this teaching. What was worse was that the teaching so perfectly suited our human carnality that people would then resist any portion of Scripture that contradicted the wrong teaching.

Second, in turning away from historic Christian theological convictions the church lost the ability to answer big questions and to articulate with clarity how Christians actually change. I was desperately concerned with having answers for skeptics regarding why we should believe the Bible, whether there were any evidences for God's existence, and other such questions. There seemed to be not only little interest in teaching these things, but outright irritation with those who insisted on getting answers and seriously discussing those subjects. This lack of clarity as to who God is and what God is doing in the world, and the unwillingness to articulate how it is that we actually change, in my view, was far more pernicious, more insidious; it was the very reversal of Christianity. It presented God as having no agenda of his own, as existing for no other reason than to serve our agendas and cater to our desire for the things of this world. I couldn't harmonize this presentation with the Bible. It seemed to actually promote what God abominated! "You adulterous people! Do you not know that friendship with the world is enmity with God? Therefore whoever wishes himself to be a friend of the world makes himself an enemy of God" (James 4:4). The more I read the Scriptures the less many of the preachers I knew looked like faithful shepherds and the more they looked like the wolves they were commissioned by Christ to guard the sheep against. Again the Scriptures are clear: "Should not shepherds feed the sheep? You eat the fat, you clothe yourselves with the wool, you slaughter the fat ones, but you do not feed the sheep" (Ezek. 34:2–3).[7]

Because of this departure from historic Christian teachings, the church was unable to adequately answer questions regarding how it is we actually change. I was very much concerned with getting deep, biblical answers for how to deal with the conflicting desires I wrestled with in my own heart. I felt that I loved God, but not enough; I felt I hated sin, but I was still drawn to it. I could very easily identify with Paul, "Wretched man that I am! Who will deliver me from this body of death?" (Rom. 7:24). I was extremely hesitant to voice my struggles, because I wasn't even sure I was supposed to have them. When I finally began to express them, I was angered that no one seemed to have a clear understanding of my struggles. Surely the Bible had a clear, consistent way of answering these questions? Some would direct me along mystical lines. If I'd pray and fast enough, I could decisively win my battle with things like lust, bitterness, anger, and other carnal impulses. I tried this, but the temptations were not only still there but seemed to grow even stronger. Others made me feel as though the answer lay in simply trying harder, but I didn't know how to try harder. Besides, this advice seemed to be condemned by the Bible itself! "These have indeed an appearance of wisdom in promoting self-made religion and asceticism and severity to the body, but they are of no value in stopping the indulgence of the flesh" (Col. 2:23).

My desperation for answers and desire for direction in transitioning into the gospel ministry led me to enroll in a program at Hartford Theological Seminary specifically designed for preparing African-Americans for ministry. That the school was equally committed to training Muslims for ministry should have sufficiently raised questions about the level of commitment to historical Christian truth lurking behind the walls of that institution. Yet, I was naive. I entered, excited about the possibility of obtaining solid ministry training.

I left the first class utterly bewildered, trying to process the professor's gleeful assertions of the Bible's supposed mistakes and general untrustworthiness in its recounting of historical events. I determined I would reject that part of his lecture and practice what my mother taught me as a child: "Son, don't believe everything your teachers tell you. Learn to swallow the meat and spit out the bones." I bent the knee in complete defeat a month later after being severely and publicly reprimanded for expressing some reservations about a section of the professor's lecture. I concluded I had better escape while I still believed that God authored the Bible![8]

I thought it best for the short term to settle in and quietly serve in my church and wait to see what God might do with me. I spent the next few years driving the church van, transporting the church's senior citizens and poorer members. It was a wonderful time, but I was unable to see that Christ was steadily leading and preparing me for future ministry. During this time I was being tempered by the Lord's senior saints, and I became better acquainted with normal church life and the struggles of the average churchgoer. God gave me a very deep love for his church and a sincere desire to see his people grow spiritually.

During this period we relocated to Fort Lauderdale, Florida, and my inner struggle and doubts went with me. I knew that God was calling me to the ministry, but I felt that I should have answers to my questions before I entered. It was during this period that God led me to a small Christian bookstore that also held regular church services. I had never before considered worshiping in such a place, as I had only attended well-established, high profile churches in the African-American community. The gentleman who ran the ministry seemed more serious than many ministers I had previously encountered and hinted that he had mentored men in the past who had gone on to become ministers. I thought that God might have a purpose for me there. In a short time I was leading a Sunday school class, and soon I was serving as youth minister, deacon, usher, and janitor. I even led the singing a few times. My questions raged on, but I realized that I no longer was asking them only for myself, but also for the people I served.

Finding Answers

Though I regularly read the Scriptures, I was drowning in questions for which I had no answers. I consulted commentaries only to discover they differed among themselves, and I wasn't sure how to decide which was right. I began again to be interested in more formal training. This time I decided to be more careful and discerning in my selection of an institution. During this period my pastor quoted the nineteenth-century English preacher Charles Haddon Spurgeon during one of his more fiery sermons. While I cannot remember the details of the sermon, it marked the opening of an entirely new chapter in my life. A short time later I inquired about Spurgeon and was directed to a book he wrote entitled *Lectures to My Students*. I had never read such a book before; I would have great difficulty expressing the strange inward delight it brought me. I sensed that I was moving toward what I had longed for since I was a child, namely a theological bedrock on which I could not only rest my faith but even build a ministry. I next read *The Pilgrim's Progress* by John Bunyan. It so excited me that I gave it to my wife, and she devoured it just as I had. I then began purchasing Spurgeon's sermons in booklet form and reading them regularly.

I made it a point to read other authors that Spurgeon favorably mentioned, including the great Puritans John Flavel, Jonathan Edwards, Robert Murray M'Cheyne, John Owen, Thomas Manton, and others. They were like enormous mountain peaks; I didn't think I could scale their heights, but I would try to climb as high as I could.

It was about this time I went public with my intentions to enroll in Trinity International University, South Florida campus. This meant that I was not going to be available to serve in my church in the same way I had previously. I was shocked and somewhat discouraged when my news wasn't favorably received and was actually spoken against. The tension was significant enough that I ended up leaving the church. I was sad but somewhat relieved, because I reasoned that this gave me the chance to find a church that would support my desire for formal education.

God led me to the historic Piney Grove First Baptist Church of Fort Lauderdale.

For the next three and a half years I lived in two distinct but equally pivotal worlds that profoundly influenced the theological course my life would take. Piney Grove First Baptist Church was a historic African-American church associated with the National Baptist Convention, an equally historic African-American denomination. Trinity International University, South Florida campus was a conservative evangelical institution associated with the Evangelical Free Church, a historically Swedish denomination. Piney Grove was 99.9 percent African-American, while Trinity was split between Caucasians, Hispanics, and blacks. Trinity was committed to imparting the tools necessary to study and teach biblical truth but not committed specifically to any one theological position. I deeply loved both church and school and was determined to be active in both settings, though at times I thought I'd collapse trying to do so.

Discovering the Five Points of Calvinism

While at Trinity I was first exposed to the five points of Calvinism, commonly referred to as TULIP.[9] The subject came up during my first Systematic Theology class and was cast in a somewhat favorable light. However, the general consensus was that only four of the points were scriptural. Limited atonement (the understanding that the atoning death of Jesus Christ was intended by God to redeem an elect group of people singled out from the perishing mass of humanity, and that it actually accomplished the salvation) was dismissed as repugnant and misrepresentative of the character of God.

Earlier I had become persuaded that limited atonement was, in fact, the true scriptural view, and that the contrary position amounted to no atonement at all and ultimately made salvation rest on what human beings did or failed to do. I couldn't see how rejecting limited atonement could square with so many of the Bible's precious statements, such as God having "saved us and called us to a holy calling, not because of our works but because

29

of his own purpose and grace, which he gave us in Christ Jesus before the ages began" (2 Tim. 1:9). For me it was not only a critical issue but a very personal one: if salvation depended finally upon anything I did or didn't do, then it was possible for me to cause my salvation to fail. Knowing myself as I did, I didn't view this as a mere possibility, but as inevitable; I would eventually fail in the Christian life. I spoke tentatively in favor of limited atonement at first, and was later ashamed of my timidity because I felt that ultimately limited atonement gave God the most glory. I felt the opposing understanding robbed God of glory by making the atonement something that only rendered men savable, but failed to actually save them until they managed on their own to respond to it. Furthermore, if someone had to be in charge of who actually went to heaven, I couldn't think of anyone better qualified to make that decision than God himself!

I began to notice that my fellow students' objections to limited atonement could be reduced to a charge of unfairness in God or a repudiation of man's free will. I realized that what was really at stake was God's absolute sovereignty in all things, and this emboldened me. The discussion grew heated one day, continued after class, and was joined by an adjunct professor who happened to be passing by. He heard my perspective and remarked to the group that I was "awfully Reformed" in my thinking. He said it kindly, and I took it as neither an insult nor a compliment. I really couldn't grasp the import of the comment, but I wanted to. That night I asked the manager of my favorite Christian bookstore where the Reformed section was, and with a puzzled look he pointed to the section I usually perused. It was the section where my favorite Puritan authors were found; I simply had not heard the term employed in the way the professor had used it.

I now began to investigate aggressively the Reformed community to discover where I might fit in. At this point I still did not actually know anyone who was Reformed. I had only read authors who had long since gone on to be with the Lord. Two events converged to alter that. First, I began to study Berkhof's *Systematic Theology* at night after my regular studies. In addition, I read Iain Murray's biography of D. Martyn Lloyd Jones.

Second, one night my wife couldn't sleep, which was a surefire sign something was troubling her. She asked, "So . . . um . . . does anyone else believe what you believe?" I thought, *Oh great, now my wife thinks I'm a heretic!* "Sure," I said, "Lloyd-Jones, Spurgeon, a guy named Jonathan Edwards. . . ." "I mean living," she replied. I told her that I was sure there were plenty of people who did, but she sounded a little doubtful.

The next day I told a friend I needed to meet some Reformed people in the area and asked who was a safe bet. I was directed to a young African-American man named Mike Campbell who had recently taken up a pastorate at Pinelands Presbyterian Church in Miami. Mike was committed to the Presbyterian Church in America (PCA) denomination and at first seemed way too enthusiastic for my comfort. Since I was not teaching that following Sunday and really wanted my wife to meet someone living and Reformed, we visited Pinelands. We were encouraged by the service. Mike gave a thorough, well-developed message that solidly explained the text and passionately applied it. My wife had a very positive experience, and I was happy. I now consciously identified myself with the Reformed movement and began sorting out where I fit within it.

After completing my studies in Miami and graduating with a BA in Biblical Studies, we relocated to Deerfield, Illinois, where I enrolled in the Masters of Divinity program at Trinity Evangelical Divinity School. As our moving truck crossed the state line between Florida and Georgia, I declared myself a Presbyterian; upon arriving in Illinois, we eventually began attending services at Lakeview Presbyterian Church, a small PCA church where we were the only African-American family. Talk about culture shock! The adjustment period was significant and not without its difficulties. My wife and I had decided that we either were going to be driven by a pursuit of truth or a desire to remain in our comfort zones. Where the two clashed, we knew we must be driven by theological conviction.

We have not looked back. We have had no need to. While I cannot pretend to have found a perfect Reformed community, I have indeed found what I had craved my entire Christian life: "a

31

reason for the hope that is within me." In the Reformed under-standing of Christianity, I learned that God has wisely incorpo-rated our earnest efforts in the process of sanctification. Sanctifi-cation is a work God himself undertakes in believers' lives, lives in which we progressively grow in holiness as we die to sin over time. As I apply myself to the Bible, prayer, and communion with the saints, I am ever to be dependent on God alone. I rejoiced to learn that my sanctification is as much by faith and a product of the death of Christ as the justification that brought me forgive-ness. I also gained a clear conception of what God is up to in his world and in my life. He is graciously summing up all things in Christ, who as God will reign eternally over God's creation, which includes his people. I learned that a day is coming, born of the obedience of Christ unto death, when all the demonic powers and world of unbelieving men will be cast into the lake of fire. God has purposed to purge and purify this very sinful world and bring into existence a new heavens and new earth wherein dwells righteousness—eternally devoid of sin, suffering, or death. I have discovered something that doesn't diminish the deep pain and travail of the world as it groans under the burden of personal and corporate sin, but that in the face of the sufferings of this present time still offers real hope that doesn't disappoint. This has given my life richness, my faith solidity, my mind inexhaustible wonders, and my heart the deepest joy imaginable.

With this understanding, I was enabled to answer God's call on my life to enter the gospel ministry, endeavoring to serve God's people and God's interest in the world. In God's good providence, I have been settled at Soaring Oaks Presbyterian Church in Elk Grove, California, and brought into connection with several like-minded African-American brothers in the faith, who, while the individual paths walked may differ, know well "the trouble I've seen."

2

From Mecca
to the Messiah

THABITI ANYABWILE

Many readers of this book will know what I mean when I say, "I grew up in small-town America."

They will instantly recognize in the notion of small-town America both the simple beauties and the strange complexities of such a setting. Small-town America is a place where "everybody knows your name," to borrow from the anthem of the '80s hit television sitcom, *Cheers*. And yet, depending on your place in that town, they're not always "glad you came." Racially, small-town America can be a place both of skin-close proximity and two worlds widely divided by a street or a track. You can work together all day or work for someone all your life, and be near strangers after 5:00 pm and on Sundays. It's a world where privacy is fiercely valued, yet there are no secrets. Small-town America is a place of long memories and sometimes short horizons.

For me, small-town America was on the whole a great place to grow up and live. But one of my most enduring memories or aspects of growing up in my cozy southern town in North Carolina was growing up without my father.

I feel the absence of my father in the most mundane moments—like the times when I need to shave in order to look presentable for some outing, only to realize I don't know how to shave. I've never learned. Before the fuzz on my face could properly be called stubble, my father had already been gone for four or five years.

The irony is that the two personal items he left behind were his razor and his shaving brush, retired in a casual lean in his 1970s yellowish-green shaving cup. I saw those items daily for several years after my father left. The fragrance from his shaving cream had long since evaporated, but the tools for a manly polished appearance were still there reminding me that he wasn't.

Growing up without my dad didn't seem all that difficult at first. Living in a small town, I would still see him from time to time. On those occasions he would give me some spending money and ask if I was doing well.

When I didn't see him, I'd sometimes get updates on his whereabouts from my older siblings or from friends who thought I'd be interested to know. Truth was, I knew where he was and what he was doing. The entire town did. And I assume they talked about it. But we rarely did in my home. No one brought it up all that much.

Dailiness took over, and life went on.

A One-Woman Boy

Perhaps the first hint that something was missing came when I grew interested in girls. I was odd for my age. Though the predominant social message and expectation for a middle schooler was "play the field," especially for us budding athletes, I wanted desperately to be a "one-woman man." I didn't know why, but I felt the desire so urgently that I think I scared a lot of nearly-pubescent girls away. Too serious way too soon.

Looking back, I tend to think that my "one-woman man" desire sprouted from the knowledge that my father and mother never married and the knowledge that he was habitually unfaithful to my mother. I witnessed the pain my mother sometimes tried to hide, and I saw the resentment welling up in the faces of my siblings, who had a different father and were old enough to understand the weight of things. At some point, I vowed that I did not want to be like my father. I did not want another mother's face to show that kind of pain. And, on some level, I began to resent him.

I'm not unique. There is a lot of "daddy pain" in the world. Approximately 70 percent of African-American children are born out of wedlock, and nearly 90 percent will spend some portion of their lives in one-parent homes, usually without a dad.

Teenagers Perish for Lack of Guidance

The second clue that something was missing came while in high school. I noticed in my best friend's relationship with his father a camaraderie I never knew. It was not simply that his dad showed up for football and basketball games, or that he gave my friend an allowance. And it wasn't that his father was married to his mother and that they all lived together; he wasn't and they didn't. What I noticed was that they were not exactly peers, but they shared in life so profoundly that it created a longing in me.

The fathers of two friends adopted me as their "son." They looked after me, encouraged me, and challenged me in some important ways. But neither man was *my* father. Neither was available whenever I needed him, and neither could be consulted in the most intimate of matters. So, I spent much of my adolescence making my own rules, seeking my own way, and consequently hurting a lot of people.

There were the loyalties I broke, the girls I defrauded, and the responsibilities I neglected. I betrayed a friend by sleeping with his girlfriend. An aborted child could have been mine; I didn't ask. And by the time I was a junior in high school, I was arrested for stealing; though at the time, I had a pocket full of money earned at my summer job. You could say I was arrested for being stupid. More precisely, though, my sins were maturing and controlling my life.

Had my father been there, perhaps I would have had someone to correct me, instruct me, to hold me responsible, and failing all, to kick my butt when necessary. At the least, I think I would have had someone to talk to, to ask questions of, and to share my life with. As it was, I was left to negotiate the most turbulent time in life without a father to guide me.

Young, Black, and Angry

All I really knew of church growing up was that whenever my brothers found themselves in trouble they "cleaned up" and "got their acts together" by going to church. They attended until their problems died down, and then gradually returned to their previous pursuits. From time to time, my mother, the only semi-regular church attender in the family, would make me go with her. I was the youngest of eight children and too young to escape my mother's efforts and sleep in on Sundays. That was church. The place you attended when your troubles overtook you or your mother made you get out of bed, dress in your one suit (a too-snug three-piece), and endure the ritual collection of middle agers and old folks.

So, it was to church that I needed to go when I was arrested. All the illusions of success in small-town North Carolina were quickly dashed as rumors spread, behaviors changed, friendships ended, and the world shrank even more. I was in trouble for the first time in my life, and I needed to "clean up." So, I began attending church.

About three Sundays into my effort to get things back on track, I decided I needed to be more committed than my seemingly always-in-trouble brothers. I decided not just to attend, but to join the church. One Sunday following the sermon I left my seat in response to an altar call and journeyed up to the big oak pulpit with the larger-than-life Bible and scarlet bookmark draping over it.

Older ladies murmured their approval as I went up front, though I didn't know why they should be pleased. A deacon, a friend of my mother's, met me at the pulpit and ushered me into a back room. "Have you ever been baptized?" he asked. "No," I said, wondering if that was part of the deal. He assured me it was and noted some things on a small index card. We went back out front where he announced that I was applying for membership "as a candidate for baptism." *Whatever,* I thought, *just as long as this thing sticks.*

About two weeks later the pastor dunked me in the baptismal pool, though I was not at all baptized in a biblical sense. In all of that time, I never heard the gospel. I was never asked if I understood what it meant to follow Jesus as Lord and Savior, or if I was repentant and trusting in Christ alone for rescue from the wrath of God. I can't even say that I knew God had any wrath against sin. I was the same person arrested a month or so earlier. In fact, when I dried off from the immersion, I rushed out of the service around the corner to the pool hall where I spent all of my time gambling and drinking. I attended church a few months or so after that, but gradually concluded that Christianity wasn't real. It had no power to change me, and Jesus, while probably a real historical figure and well-intentioned, had little he could do for me.

For most of my junior and senior years in high school, I skulked through the halls swinging in mood from anger to depression to indifference. Not many people noticed. Or, if they did, they didn't say much. My grades remained high. I continued on the basketball team. And I made the social rounds at football games and after-parties.

One teacher who did notice, an eccentric middle-aged Jewish lady transplanted by marriage from some northern state, tried to befriend me (as a fellow alien perhaps) and give me something positive to do with my anger. She introduced me to the writings of a number of 1960s radicals—Amiri Baraka, Stokely Carmichael, Gwendolyn Brooks, Malcolm X, and others. It was a well-intended effort, I think. But giving an angry kid the incendiary writings of angry adults is a little like giving a pyromaniac free gasoline and a box of matches along with a top-ten list for why the world should go up in flames.

I grew angrier—silently angry at a father who had left a few years earlier, angry at friends who distanced themselves from me because of my arrest, angry at "fake" Christians and the church, and angry at people in general. I stayed this way until I went off to college.

Mecca Found and Abandoned

My college roommate was my best friend from high school. He and I arrived at college with barely any supplies for school, two cases of beer, and ready for the college party life. My best semester in college was my first semester, which was a minor miracle since a good bit of the time I was drinking.

But by the second semester of my freshman year, dissatisfaction rooted itself in my heart. Life was empty. The routine bored me, and I yearned for more, though I didn't know what.

Having started reading '60s radicals in high school, I continued to read everything available about African and African-American history and culture. I devoured the stuff, angry that my high school education so dismissively skipped over this part of my identity and history. Marcus Garvey, Malcolm X, and Martin R. Delaney became heroes. I wanted very much to be a Garvey or Malcolm to my own generation.

I committed myself to the Afro-centric ideal and spent those formative college years attempting to see the world from the distinct vantage point of African people, to be African-centered. Names like Molefi Asante, John S. Mbiti, Yosef Ben-Jochannan, Ivan Van Sertima, Na'im Akbar, and Wade Nobles dotted my bookshelves and shaped my thinking about African peoples and the world. As the president of a student group called the Society of African-American Culture, I had the opportunity to host many of these men and others at campus events. Through these authors and others, I tried my best to identify a "return address" and to chart a return route to an ancestral history lost to me. I had mail to deliver and hoped they had been saving family letters and heirlooms for me.

One day, several striking men appeared at a campus lecture. They were clean-shaven, well-dressed, upright. They spoke of the African-American community and the need for black men to be *men*—to clean up, to lead and care for their families, and to live devout spiritual lives.

They enthralled me. I'd never seen black men like these—confident, focused, and somehow able to channel their anger into a cause. I discovered they were Muslims, members of the Nation of Islam, which I had read so much about as I studied Malcolm X and the history of the Civil Rights Movement. I wanted to be like them; I wanted to be manly. I wanted to fill that hole left by my own father's absence.

I ended up befriending a couple of these men, learning from them what I could. To their disappointment, I learned enough to know that the Nation of Islam was a cult and not true Islam. For the rest of my freshman year I learned as much as I could about Islam from reading and from friends.

My sophomore year in college a classmate returned from summer vacation dressed in traditional Muslim garb. While spending time with an uncle in New Jersey, he converted to a more orthodox brand of Islam. He asked us to call him Fahim, his new Muslim name, and he disavowed the rowdy life we had all lived during our freshman year.

Studying with Fahim gave me enough understanding and courage to convert to Islam. We reflected together on the pillars of Islam, prayer, and the Qur'an. For me Islam was the answer to the discipline, the brotherhood, and the longing for adult male leadership that had eluded me since age fourteen. Its promise of a simply-understood God, of a philosophy and discipline that provided for all of life's needs, and of a universal religion for all men made sense to me.

For months I met with Fahim and others studying the claims of Islam. I believed what we might call the meta-narrative of Islam. Islam maintained that it was the final and seal of all religions, that a certain progression from Judaism to Christianity to Islam could be observed in history. Accordingly, the Prophet Muhammad was the final and seal of all the prophets, bringing the most perfect revelation of all, the Qur'an. I believed the "simpler" revelation of Islam, that there is but one God, Allah, Muhammad his messenger, and Jesus merely a prophet. Islam removed the mystery of the Trinity and the wonder of a sinless God-man who died for the sins of the world. Its initial attraction was the combination of its claims to simplicity and logic and its offer of a discipline for all of life.

The night I converted to Islam was an emotional one. I sat across the dorm room bed from the young woman who would eventually become my wife. I told her with a rush of joy and resolve that I had decided to become a Muslim. She had seen it coming, but to my surprise and hers she wept in grief at the news. That night, despite her tears, I recited the Shahaddah: "There is no God but Allah, and Muhammad is his messenger." I was Muslim.

Zealous for Islam, I spoke of it whenever and wherever I could. I introduced several fellow students to the teachings of the Qur'an and helped them to enter the faith as well. Five times a day I prayed facing Mecca. I rose early to study the Qur'an and other Islamic literature. I fasted during Ramadan, served the community, and lived a devout and faithful Muslim life to the best of my ability.

After about a year, using a book of African names, I settled on a new name: Thabiti Montsho Anyabwile. The name captured what I hoped to become. "Thabiti" is a Swahili name that comes from the Arabic root word "thabit," meaning "upright, stern." In the Swahili context it loosely translates "true man." A lifelong need now bloomed into an ambition. "Montsho" means "black" and "Anyabwile" means "God has set me free." Life was ordered, purposeful . . . and fueled by a growing anger, this time at overly patriotic (that is, patriotic at all) white Americans, and Christians who hid the truth of Allah.

I opposed the cross of Jesus Christ with all my might. I regarded the crucifixion a big myth, a hoax, a lie perpetrated against weaker-minded, less-informed, sentimental people. I rejected the Bible as a corrupted book, and insisted that Jesus was only a prophet—and a black-skinned Muslim one at that. Whenever Christian students passed out tracts or street preachers came near campus, I heckled and harassed them. I desired to overthrow the faith of anyone calling themselves "Christians." I had found the truth in Islam and purposed that everyone else should discover it as well.

Babylon . . . Again

This was my life for the remainder of undergraduate school and a year or so after graduation. But gradually, almost imperceptibly at first, I noticed that I was growing more and more hollow. Cold, really. The zeal once fueled by anger began to wane. Once adjusted to all the rituals and outward observances of Islam, I grew more aware of my interior life.

Awareness of the emptiness of my own heart grew crystal clear for me after a water cooler conversation with co-workers about people we admired and respected. Folks were listing the usual suspects: mothers, fathers, great leaders, and so on. But surprisingly, one co-worker said with all seriousness, "I can't think of a more righteous person than Thabiti." I dismissed her statement with some light response of my own. But she countered, "I'm dead serious. Of all the men I know, you are easily the most righteous. You don't curse. You don't drink. You treat your wife well." And on she went.

I was taken aback, stunned really.

While I didn't curse or drink anymore, and I tried to treat my wife Kristie well, my co-worker's conclusion seemed ridiculous to me. What she observed was outward behavior; what she couldn't see was my heart. But I could, and the thing was as brittle and empty as it could be. The label "righteous" fell into all of that deep emptiness, rattling occasionally as it plummeted and banged against the hull of my heart. One thing I knew: I was not righteous, not in any essential sense.

And increasingly, I grew aware that I could not be righteous. I made prayer faithfully—even developed a dark patch on my forehead from bowing onto my prayer carpet. I read the Qur'an actively. I did all I could, but no righteousness, no essential change resulted. My anger, lusts, hatred, and evil thoughts were all still with me.

During Ramadan, the Islamic month of fasting and prayer, I rose from bed well before sunrise and morning prayer to read the Qur'an, studying it for solutions for my troubled conscience and heart. As I poured over the pages, however, all I found were contradictions and half truths. The Qur'an taught that Jesus was virgin born (Surah 3:45–48; 19:20ff) and that he was helped by the Holy Spirit (Surah 2:87, 253). The Qur'an and the Hadith taught that Jesus was faultless. And some eleven times the Qur'an referred to Jesus as "the Messiah."

41

How could Jesus be virgin born, helped by the Holy Spirit, faultless, the Messiah, and not be the Son of God, a member of the Trinity, and the Savior that the Old Testament prophets looked for? Every Muslim believes that Jesus is a prophet, and that a prophet speaks the very words of God, and that the Torah, Psalms of David, and the Gospels were revelations from Allah. How could I consistently hold that view and reject Jesus' teachings about himself and the way to eternal life?

I couldn't. But rather than bend the knee in worship to Jesus, I threw up my hands and renounced all religion. On my best days, I was an agnostic; on my worst days, I toyed with atheism. I was empty, confused, arrogant, and lost . . . again.

False Hope

I lived a lost, God-rejecting, self-seeking life for about a year. Not surprisingly, my marriage grew empty as well, and the difficulties started to appear overwhelming.

Then, my wife and I learned that we were pregnant with our first child. Our families were ecstatic. We began to feel a sense of hope and anticipation, daydreaming about a white house with a picket fence and the gentle coos of a new child. We began to build our lives on this dream.

Three months into the pregnancy, we visited the doctor's office for a regular visit. It was to be the first visit where we heard the baby's heartbeat. Our excitement made it nearly impossible to sit patiently in the waiting room. We flitted through magazines, squeezed one another's hand, and chatted incessantly about the details of baby's arrival.

Finally, we entered the examination room, where Kristie promptly readied herself for the exam. The doctor entered, mostly ignoring me, and began her work. After a few minutes, making several different attempts to find the baby's heartbeat, she spoke in the most lifeless, spiritless, barren human voice I've ever heard. "I'm sorry. There's no heartbeat. The baby is dead."

My wife wept inconsolably. I stood frozen. My feet grew roots and planted me in the floor. My brittle heart cracked, and in flooded a message that seemed to fill my entire head. I did not expect or understand it. I "heard" simply, "Son, come home."

Coming Home to Calvary

Following the miscarriage, my wife and I tried to keep moving on with life. She returned to teaching after a week or so, but I mostly sat around the house depressed. For weeks, that message rang in my head, "Son, come home."

It was an odd, hazy time. Numbness and rawness took turns at mastering my thoughts and feelings.

Yet, on several occasions I found myself in traffic behind a car with "John 1:12" printed on the license plate. I recognized it was from the Bible, but I didn't know the verse. I tried to put it out of my head.

One Tuesday morning, two hours late for work but casually flipping through television channels, I landed on the weekly broadcast of a church service. I couldn't explain why I stopped to listen, but I did. Strangely, the words had life. They beckoned me. It wasn't even a particularly evangelistic sermon. The preacher simply expounded on Paul's words to Timothy: "Study to show yourself approved." But those words gripped me.

For a couple of months, I taped the show and watched it with my wife. We learned that the pastor's church was located in the Washington, D.C. area, where my wife's sister lived. We decided to visit her sister and the church.

That Sunday morning, we were among the first to enter the church. We sat directly in front of the pulpit about five rows back. It seemed that half of the church's twenty-two thousand members packed out this first service. But God intended every word spoken that morning from Exodus 32 especially for me. The pastor titled the sermon, "What Does It Take to Make You Angry?" Tailor-made, it was a careful and convicting look at sin and idolatry and the consequences of sin. It was a challenge to develop a righteous, godly indignation toward sin, to hate sin and to turn to God.

Every sin, every act of idolatry, every wicked attitude mentioned that morning described me. The preacher expounded the

Law, and I saw my need for a Savior, someone to rescue me from the wrath of God against sin. I sat gripped as the holiness and justice of God were unfolded from Scripture. I grew strangely remorseful and alert, awakened really, as the pastor applied the doctrine of sin to his hearers. I was convicted, guilty before this holy God who judges all unrighteousness.

Then, with plain yet beautiful speech, the preacher exalted Jesus for us to see. Here was the Lamb of God for us to behold! He made it clear that Jesus was the Son of God sent by the Father to die as a substitute for all who would turn from their sins, renouncing them, and turn toward God through faith in Jesus. Here was the Sacrifice anticipated in the Old Testament and executed in the New. Here in Jesus was redemption. The sinless Son of God had indeed come into the world to save everyone who believes—even a former Muslim who was an avowed and determined enemy of the cross!

For the first time, I longed to know God. I longed to know Jesus. I longed to be saved from the misery of sin and the life controlled by it.

"Repent and believe for the forgiveness of your sins" came the invitation. In God's kindness, my wife and I were given the gift of repentance and faith, turning from our sins and to Jesus in faith on that day. In God's mercy, the stranglehold of years of anger and hatred were broken literally overnight. The gospel triumphed where no other power had or could.

The Doctrines of Grace

My wife and I returned to North Carolina full of wonder and joy. We were changed. The world sparkled with a newness and freshness we didn't know was available. Everything was lovely.

As undergraduate students, we had owned and operated a bookstore specializing in African and African-American titles. We loved books. And so our instinct told us to visit a Christian bookstore and find something good to read. That Monday we visited a local bookstore and browsed the shelves. Being something of a history buff, and feeling the embarrassment of having believed what I came to regard as a complete falsehood, I wandered back to the couple of shelves on theology and church history.

Two titles screamed at me from the shelves: *Knowing God* and *Great Doctrines of the Bible.* I didn't know J. J. Packer or D. Martyn Lloyd-Jones from Adam, but I left the store with these volumes happily tucked under my arm. I devoured the books, imbibing the great truths of Reformed Christianity unawares.

I giggle to myself when I recall my attitude and margin notes reading these books. When I hit comments on predestination, for example, I'd write, "Who is this guy? The rest of this book is basically pretty good, but this predestination stuff is crazy." I had no categories for Reformed thought, and so I reflexively defended what I had heard from so many pulpits and televangelists. Surely they could not all be incorrect; we choose God, right?

Nevertheless, Lloyd-Jones and Packer became favorite authors. I read some of their other books, all the while acquiring more understanding of Scripture. Two conversations provided the spark for connecting the dots of my theological commitments.

About three years into my new life with Christ, I asked a church leader what he thought about predestination. He was a long-time Christian worker with a large parachurch organization. I respected his opinion theologically. He sort of laughed and said, "Doctor (he called everybody "Doctor") . . . that's that Reformed theology stuff. How God's sovereignty fits with man's freedom and stuff. Man, I don't mess around in that deep stuff." With that, I was determined to play in what he called the deeper end of the theological pool.

A little while later, a dear childhood friend and I began to study Scripture together. He was an older Christian with Prosperity Gospel and charismatic commitments. Eventually, he raised questions about eternal security. He took the position that a born-again man could "lose his salvation." That made little sense to me. We corresponded by e-mail several times a week and invited other friends into the discussion. I decided I had better solve this in my own mind once and for all.

Back to the bookstore I went. I decided to read the best things I could find from both positions. The Lord lead me to Norman

Geisler's *Chosen but Free*, R. C. Sproul's *Willing to Believe* and *What Is Reformed Theology?*[1] Martin Luther's *The Bondage of the Will*, and A. W. Pink's *The Sovereignty of God*. I read *Chosen but Free* and *What Is Reformed Theology?* By the time I finished Sproul's books and *The Sovereignty of God*, I was a convinced advocate of Reformed theology. That is to say, I was convinced that Reformed theology was a nickname for biblical theology.

Sproul's *What Is Reformed Theology?* provided the skeletal outline for a more complete understanding of the "five *solas*" and the acrostic "TULIP." Pink's *The Sovereignty of God* provided the flesh for a big understanding of the nature and work of God. After finishing these works, I was on my knees in awe of the Lord Almighty, Creator and Ruler of all things.

Now the massive glory and awesomeness of God emerged for me as I read the Bible. That God was sovereign in all things meant he was completely trustworthy in all things. That he was sovereign in electing me unto salvation meant that his love was free and my salvation secure. Election and predestination became the grounds for my confidence in God's rescue of me from sin and wrath and preservation for eternity. Christ's death accomplished the Father's purposes for me; he made atonement for my sins and made my redemption certain, not possible.

With the Scripture unveiled and God standing supreme over all things, I wondered how I could ever have believed otherwise. Surely, that angry young man would not have chosen the things of God by his own desires. That angry Muslim opposed to the cross would not have come to Christ by his own devotion and zeal. The fledgling agnostic-atheist could not reason his way to the Lord. My redemption from start to finish was and is all of God—by his grace alone, through the gift of faith alone, in the wonderful Savior Son of God, Jesus Christ alone, for the glory of God alone. And I am grateful, deeply grateful.

3

Clemson University Saved My Life

ANTHONY B. BRADLEY

Atlanta

I used to wonder why so many blacks in the South are either Baptists or Methodists. Looking at the history of the southern church it soon became quiet clear to me: those denominations were the only ones that showed great interest in (and were successful at) reaching "Negroes." It is from the Baptist/Methodist context that I come. Both my parents were raised in the Baptist church. My grandfather on my father's side was a Baptist preacher. When my parents moved to the suburbs of Atlanta in the early 1970s, they started attending Ben Hill United Methodist Church (which recently peaked at over ten thousand members). Ben Hill is where my journey into Reformed theology begins.

In the United Methodist Church I was nurtured into the sacramental theology of the followers of John Wesley. "The Wesleyan emphasis upon the Christian life—faith and love put into practice—has been the hallmark of those traditions now incorporated into The United Methodist Church (UMC). The distinctive shape of the Wesleyan theological heritage can be seen in a constellation of doctrinal emphases that display the creating, redeeming, and sanctifying activity of God."[1] Wesley and the early Methodists were particularly concerned about inviting people to experience God's grace and to grow in their knowledge and love of God through disciplined Christian living. They placed primary emphasis on putting faith and love into action. This emphasis on what Wesley referred to as "practical divinity" continues to be a way that United Methodists understand themselves as distinct from other denominations. The United Methodist Church says, "The distinctive shape of our theological heritage can be seen not only in this emphasis on Christian living, but also in Wesley's distinctive understanding of God's saving grace. Although Wesley shared with many other Christians a belief in salvation by grace, he combined them in a powerful way to create distinctive emphases for living the full Christian life."[2]

At Ben Hill I was introduced to the liturgical calendar. I was an acolyte (an altar boy) for most of my early life, so I was always wearing robes and colorful vestments according to the specifications of the liturgical calendar. I love robes. I felt important wearing one. All the pastors had robes. I had a robe. I knew I was part of an ancient tradition, something historical. I used to imagine myself wearing a robe and preaching. In fact, they still wear robes at Ben Hill, and I love that about the church. The baby boomers did not corrupt that part of their liturgy.

My pastor was Cornelius Henderson. Dr. Henderson later became a bishop in the United Methodist Church and was a great man. The Interdenominational Theological Center in Atlanta even named a building after him. One day, Dr. Henderson came over to our house to take me to lunch at Hardees. I've never forgotten that. How many megachurch pastors take random middle school kids out to lunch? He was a wonderful pastor.

I think there is a large part of me that preaches like Dr. Henderson—at least I hope so. Looking back, I recognize that he practiced the essence of homiletics: applying the Scriptures to our real, day-to-day encounters with the brokenness in this world. At Ben Hill sermons were not three-point theology lectures with three brief sentences of non-specific application at the end like, "God is faithful," "stop sinning," or "trust God." The sermons I heard growing up (and didn't appreciate at the time) were honest attempts to apply truth to struggle.

I sure hated the music there, though. We sung hymn after hymn after hymn, in between the corporate recitation of confessions and various creeds. I'm not certain how many teenage boys would say they love hymns; none would be my guess. Instead, I liked the upbeat gospel music with the drums, the Hammond B-3 organ, and everything else. I loved the foot-stomping, hand-clapping, crowd-swaying, indigenous expressions of a community's walk with God as it enjoyed sacramental life together. But "we were Methodists," I was told. We didn't do things like "others" did (and by that we meant the Baptists, who conducted worship in a very disorderly fashion). Ours was an all-black church that was very "high church."

In an honest moment I will admit that my love of liturgy and my view that Christianity and social justice concerns are inseparable comes from my Methodist upbringing. Looking back I appreciate the Methodists who put their lives on the line to fight against slavery and, later, white supremacy in the South. For example, Methodist minister and Tennessee governor William Gannaway Brownlow, after getting his bearings straight on slavery, fought to eradicate the Klu Klux Klan from the state during Reconstruction, while leaders in other denominations were silent, secretly promoted the activities, or turned a blind eye.

When I graduated from high school I did not know any evangelical lingo. If anyone had asked me, "How does someone become a Christian?" I would have said, "Uh, go to church?" I was certainly a soft Universalist and believed that all religions eventually led to the God of the Bible. I knew very little about the Bible and very little about a life of repentance and faith. I had no commitments to the inerrancy and infallibility of the Scriptures. My church simply did not discuss such matters.

Clemson

In the fall of 1989 I arrived at Clemson University to embark on an experience that would forever change my life. I lived on the eighth floor in C-section of the Johnstone dormitory, room 826. Down the hall was a kid named Graham from South Jersey (Cherry Hill, to be exact). He had become a Christian through a high school campus ministry called Young Life. We were both biology majors and had many classes together. Graham and I became fast friends. Or, rather, I tagged along with him a lot. Graham came to Clemson with his best friend, Derek. I would try to hang around them as much as I could. I wasn't sure why, but these were some of the coolest guys I had ever met. They introduced me to Monty Python movies. The first one I saw was *Monty Python and the Holy Grail*. I didn't get the humor at first, which led me to think that white guys liked weird stuff. Monty Python was not popular in my black, middle-class neighborhood.

While I was a student (at the best university in the world), I was blessed to be immersed in a campus with thirteen Christian ministries. There were several people who bounced back and forth between Fellowship of Christian Athletes (FCA), Reformed University Fellowship (RUF), and Campus Crusade for Christ. The Crusade guys were after me big time. They hounded me with the "Four Spiritual Laws." To get them off my trail, once when they visited my dorm room I played "Jesus Is Just Alright with Me" by the Doobie Brothers. It didn't work.

Graham and Derek were different. No pressure, no laws, just love and community. I was certainly converted to community before I became a committed Jesus-follower. Maybe the Crusade guys should have just asked me to go hang out. Derek and Graham were amazing because they were open to letting this black dude hang out with them while they went to all this Christian stuff on campus.

The first time I went to an FCA meeting, I was blown away. I had never seen anything like it. Hundreds and hundreds of people were singing songs I had never heard of accompanied by some dudes playing acoustic guitars. I had never seen acoustic guitars played within the context of worship. The FCAers carried their Bibles everywhere. They were clothed in their Jesus T-shirts and wore crosses around their necks, and they wore flip-flops year-round. It was an odd culture shock. I was not sure that they understood that being like Jesus did not mean that all Christian guys had to wear ten-dollar flip-flops, Tevas, or Burkenstocks every day.

My first couple of years with FCA I was "saved" several times. I walked down the aisle a few times, or at least felt convicted and wanted to, because I felt guilty about something I had done and wanted to turn my life around. I wanted to go to heaven and didn't want to burn in hell because of my sin. At FCA I learned that sinners go to hell if they don't repent. I sinned a lot, so I wanted to walk down the aisle frequently. I didn't know any other way to handle my guilt.

One night later in my freshman year, I walked down the aisle, and I meant it. That was it. I was done. I knew I needed help. I wanted to be close to God, but I didn't know how. So I walked down the aisle, said the "sinner's prayer," and went backstage to meet with my "counselor." I was told that this "counselor" was going to help me learn about Christianity and teach me the ropes. That didn't happen. I walked behind stage, was welcomed into the kingdom, met my "counselor," prayed for about three minutes, and didn't see the dude again for four years (right before I graduated I ran into him, and he apologized for dropping me like that). I was so confused. You walk down the aisle, say the prayer, get a spiritual "counselor," and then once "you're in," you get dropped like a subprime mortgage. I now realize what I needed was something called "discipleship." I felt strange. It was as if the whole point of the night was to get me to come down the aisle and say the prayer. The rest was up to me.

Sadly, since I wasn't experiencing the "wonderful life" I was promised, and since no one helped me learn, I went back to living how I was before. Hello, Coors Extra Gold!

Graham also took me to Reformed University Fellowship (RUF), which is the college ministry of the Presbyterian Church in America. David Sinclair was the campus minister in those days. He is now Dr. David Sinclair, and is the senior pastor of one the most amazing churches in all of Christianity: Clemson Presbyterian Church. There was something unusual about the teaching at RUF; David's teaching was different from any of the FCA speakers I had heard. At the time, I had no idea what exactly it was. I did know that he didn't do a lot of yelling and sweating, and I really liked that.

RUF was a bit smaller, with about three hundred people. Coming from my church background, this was a small gathering. It seems to me that if you're going to have a college ministry to reach the nations on a college campus, one would want it to be the largest organization on campus. Not because "bigger is better," but because bigger means greater influence on the campus. If you are there to truly bring redemption to the campus, praying for as many people to join as possible seems like a good thing. I've heard that there are some college campus leaders who actually want to keep their ministries small, which seems to be contrary to the missional identity of the people of God (Gen. 12:2).

But Clemson's RUF was a good crowd and thankfully a fairly large one. There were RUF students involved in all sorts of activities and organizations on campus. In RUF you could be a Christian and still remain in your fraternity. I loved that position. I was a member of the Alpha Phi Alpha fraternity and did not want to leave it. You were not encouraged to withdraw from the world, thereby submitting to unbiblical distinctions between the sacred and secular. The RUF people were cool to me, too. Like FCA, they worshiped with acoustic guitars, which, looking back, still seems odd. But I began to see that perhaps God might accept the worship of people who weren't clapping "on two" and were missing the Hammond B-3 organ.

During my senior year, after three years of bouncing back and forth between "normal" Division-I football culture, my fraternity, my friend's fraternity (somehow I became an honorary Sigma Chi), FCA, RUF, and a small crisis after failing to be admitted to Tiger Brotherhood (a prestigious Clemson organization), I finally became a committed follower of Jesus. And that is when everything changed. I got it (sort of). I finally realized what all that repentance talk was about and why people wore Jesus T-shirts and prayed in public in circles holding hands. I understood why people were singing songs to Jesus backed by acoustic guitars. I understood why people lifted their hands into the air during worship (although I don't really lift my own hands except when listening to the Josh Moyer Band from Pittsburgh). My eyes were finally opened.

Reformation at Clemson

The first thing I did after committing my life to following Jesus was join something called a "Bible study." I had never been to one before. I was not aware of such Bible studies in my church while I was growing up, though I am sure they existed. I don't recall my family ever going to them. My first Bible study was lead by David Sinclair. We studied the first eight chapters of the book of Romans for an entire semester. It was amazing—three and a half months on eight chapters. I didn't know this was possible.

I brought my RSV (Revised Standard Version) to the Bible study at first. It was the Bible I received from Ben Hill on June 19, 1989, when I graduated from high school. I still have that Bible today and read it for my devotions. After a few weeks I noticed that everyone else had a different Bible. My RSV had slightly different words. I was confused, and I couldn't follow along, so I went and purchased something called the "New International Version." The evangelical world was so foreign to me, I didn't even know about the "old international version."

The Romans Bible study changed my life. It was the first time I had ever read the list of sins in Romans 1 and realized that I was one of the people Paul was talking about. I knew I had lied about and slandered someone at least three times in my life! I also learned about "justification" (Rom. 3:23). The definition went something like this: "Just-as-if-I'd-never-sinned-and-lived-a-perfect-life." This is how God looks at me because of what Jesus accomplished on the cross and in his resurrection. Wow! I was completely and fully justified before God because of my faith in Christ. It was not because of the goods things that I did, but because of the perfect life that Jesus lived. Grace was amazing.

The Westminster Larger Catechism has two wonderful questions that help to unpack the biblical teaching on justification:

Question 70: What is justification?

Answer: Justification is an act of God's free grace unto sinners, in which he pardons all their sins, accepts and accounts their persons righteous in his sight; not for anything wrought in them, or done by them, but only for the perfect obedience and full satisfaction of Christ, by God imputed to them, and received by faith alone.

Question 73: How does faith justify a sinner in the sight of God?

Answer: Faith justifies a sinner in the sight of God, not because of those other graces which do always accompany it, or of good works that are the fruits of it, nor as if the grace of faith, or any act thereof, were imputed to him for his justification; but only as it is an instrument by which he receives and applies Christ and his righteousness.

This justification information was very encouraging and liberating. Saved by grace, not by works (Eph. 2:8–10)! I wanted everyone to hear about this, even if I had to argue with them.

During my senior year I devoured the Scriptures, especially the New Testament. I couldn't get enough. I miss being a young Christian. There were so many wonderful things to discover in the first eight chapters of Romans. I have that Bible in front of me as I write this chapter, and I wrote so many phrases in any available white space. On the Romans 7 page I wrote, "Non-Christians do not struggle with sin." Sinclair must have said that. I've been teaching a variation on that theme ever since. If you don't have the Holy Spirit, you're not going to struggle with wanting to be conformed to the image of Jesus Christ.

The second study I did with Sinclair (or Master Yoda) was a book study of *Putting Amazing Back into Grace: An Intro-*

duction to Reformed Theology, by Michael Scott Horton. I was completely blown away. I learned so much about the history of the church, about John Calvin, the Canons of Dort, the Reformed *solas*, and a flower called "TULIP." I learned about Martin Luther. I liked him a lot. He was a straight shooter who called a spade a spade. Horton's book became the scaffolding for understanding the loftier doctrines of the Reformed world. I was most captivated, though, by the *solas* and the flower of the Reformation era:

1. *Scripture alone:* Scripture is God's Word and is the final authority for our faith and practice (2 Tim. 3:16).
2. *Christ alone:* Salvation comes to sinners only through the person and work of Jesus Christ (John 5:24).
3. *Grace alone:* God's redeeming work in his creation comes to us freely, as a gift (Eph. 2:1–8).
4. *Faith alone:* No works, no status, no power can achieve salvation from God; we are saved by trusting in Jesus as Lord and Savior (Eph. 2:8–9).
5. *God's glory alone:* God, and God alone, has done a great work in redeeming his creation and saving his people, therefore all glory belongs to him (Rev. 5:13).

I also greatly appreciated being instructed about TULIP, which I have modified from James Montgomery Boice's teaching:[3]

T represents total depravity (Rom. 3:10–12). This does not mean that all persons are as evil as they have the potential to be at every moment, but rather that all human beings are affected by sin in every area of thought and conduct so that apart from the regenerating grace of God one cannot live a life that is pleasing to God.

U represents unconditional election (2 Thess. 2:13). Beginning in the Pentateuch, God has chosen to redeem those who would perish apart from his sovereign choice and mighty acts, not based on any condition man can fulfill on his own but upon God's grace alone.

L represents limited atonement (Rom. 8:30). A better name for this would be particular atonement. It is the idea that the atoning work of the Savior applies particularly to those whom the Father brings to the Son.

I represents irresistible grace (John 10:14–15). When God changes our hearts, regenerating us, creating a renewed will within, and turning us toward him, what was formerly undesirable becomes a highly desirable new passion, and we run to the cross of Christ instead of living a life running from him.

P represents perseverance of the saints (Phil. 1:6). It is God who perseveres with his people, keeping us from falling away from him. The grace that saves is the same grace that carries us through this life and the next. God's persevering work in our lives reminds us of our election.

Now that I was fully armed with Romans and the slogans of the Reformed faith, I was ready to do battle with the enemy: the "Arminians." I did not know where Arminia was, but I knew that its theology spoke of sinful people "finding Jesus" and people "choosing" Jesus by their own sin-shackled "free will." Since I knew that the Scriptures never used those terms (there is no "free will" verse), I was prepared to convert these "Arminians."

I also learned that the topic of "predestination" was one that often led to late nights spent lingering in the dining hall, arguments, shouting, and Christians not loving one another. Those were lively discussions and sometimes led to people being converted to what many of us students considered the absolute truth: Reformed theology. I remember Sinclair having to rebuke us one night because we were causing some disunity amongst the Christians on campus. It was sad. We Christians were fighting about the details of the mystery of salvation, and meanwhile the devil was wreaking havoc in Tiger Land.

The Fall Break That Sealed the Deal

A few months before I graduated I was completely lost vocationally. I had decided not to go to medical school, but had no idea what else to do. As a political junkie I considered maybe getting a PhD in public policy, but I also loved the theology I was learning. Back in those days I would walk around with a Bible, the Westminster Confession of Faith, and a copy of the United States Constitution. What else does a man need to fight "the liberals" at every turn? I was always ready to quote from the Bible or either of the two nearly canonical documents (to my young mind).

One night at RUF Sinclair had laryngitis, which might have been God's way of helping him take a break from teaching so much. He asked for people to come up and share anything God had laid upon their hearts—which I thought was so un-Presbyterian and unregulative. But the Lord laid a burden on my heart to tell my friends about their need to read the Bible.

"Guys," I preached. "You know when you brush your teeth and everything looks good and you're satisfied? But then you start flossing between your teeth and you find all the gunk and food that your toothbrush missed? The Bible works like that," I said. "Just when you think you're okay, you read the Bible and realize that you've got some sin and junk deep in your heart that needs to be picked out." I concluded my little sermonette with the idea that it is the Word of God that reveals the depths of our need for Jesus. If we leave our self-perception to ourselves, we will live lives of self-deception.

After that talk, people started saying that I needed to go to seminary. I thought, *you're nuts!* And, *how much money can I make being a preacher?* I still had some residual "old nature" stuff to work through.

A few weeks later during fall break a group from Clemson took a road trip to St. Louis to tour the campus of Covenant Theological Seminary. I went with them only because I love road trips, and I wanted to see St. Louis. I had no intention of seriously looking at the school.

When we arrived on campus, we went into the bookstore. My eyes were drawn to an orange book about ten feet up, about as thick as a telephone book, with the word "justification" covering the length of the entire spine. The clouds opened. I heard a choir of women singing an A-sharp harmony. Sunlight burst through the ceiling. There was an entire book on one word? How could that be?

At some point during that same semester I met John Sowell, who was working for Westminster Seminary in California. He invited me to apply. So, after being sucked into a group of guys who were all going to seminary—most of my closest friends from my freshman year—I applied to both Covenant and Westminster.

I had originally decided to go to Westminster, but lack of money was a big obstacle. I had left Atlanta and the black church with only $500 to my name. I needed help. I had no one from whom to "raise support" to attend an all-white, Reformed seminary. I'll never forget dropping the bomb on John when I told him I wasn't coming to Westminster after all. I felt bad, but California was a long way from Atlanta, and I had only five hundred bucks.

In the end, I chose Covenant. They had on-campus housing and much needed, and appreciated, scholarship money. Not to mention that Kevin Teasley, my admissions contact, called me, it seemed, every week for months before I arrived on campus.

Before leaving for seminary in early 1994, I joined Intown Community Church (PCA) in Atlanta and became a member of the Presbyterian Church in America. My United Methodist days were officially over.

From Student to Teacher

I enrolled in Covenant Seminary in the fall of 1994 to pursue a Master of Divinity degree. And it was tough! I had only been a committed Jesus-follower for two years; I didn't know much about the Bible; there weren't many black people around; and there were more fans of the Confederate Battle Flag than I expected. I knew nothing about southern Presbyterian history. I learned quickly.

I excelled in theology, thanks to RUF, and had to play catch-up in my Biblical Studies courses. My studies were rigorous, the community life was unmatched, and the school's emphasis on grace and solid expository preaching reconfigured my heart and mind.

The professors knew me personally, and I really appreciated that. Starting at Covenant was also the beginning of my career in youth ministry, in which I am still heavily involved today.

During my last seminary year, Dr. David Jones, now Professor Emeritus of Systematic Theology and Ethics, asked me if I had considered pursuing a PhD. I actually had been thinking about it, but since PhDs and books are the idols of a seminary student I had decided not to pursue it unless there was external confirmation to do so. Dr. Jones provided "the sign," so I decided to pursue PhD studies in theology at Westminster Theological Seminary in Philadelphia. I wanted to get deeply rooted in Reformed theology since I had only been a committed Jesus-follower for two years before entering seminary.

After finishing my coursework at Westminster I was off to work at a think tank called the Acton Institute for the Study of Religion and Liberty in Grand Rapids, Michigan. After three years of freezing cold temperatures and snow I accepted an invitation to return to Covenant and began teaching systematic theology there in the fall of 2005.

So What?

Reformed theology has been a journey in the discovery of my true identity, community, mission, and freedom. The grace of God rescued me from the penalty of sin, united me to Christ, and restored my humanity in his image. It sent me out into the world for kingdom mission in community with the body of his people until Jesus returns for the consummation of the kingdom and final restoration of creation.

If the doctrines of grace do not inform how one understands coming to Christ, remaining in Christ, and being with him in glory forever, the Christian life becomes oppressive, legalistic, and dead. The grace that saves is the same grace that sanctifies, calls us into kingdom mission, and causes us to persevere through this present age and into the age to come.

Reformed theology avoids unbiblical dichotomies regarding the scope of redemption. There are many who have a Calvinistic view of salvation but do not have a Reformed view of creation and culture—that is, a reformational world and lifeview. As such, redemption is reduced to the salvation of souls and ignores the cosmic scope of Christ's redeeming all of creation.

Albert Wolters explains that all of creation is included in the scope of redemption: "It is *all* of creation that is included in the scope of redemption. . . . Through Christ, God determined 'to reconcile to himself *all things*,' writes Paul (Col. 1:20), and the words he uses (*ta panta*) preclude any narrow or personal understanding of the reconciliation he has in mind."[4] Following Jesus, then, is being an intimate kingdom ally with God and understanding one's role in his cosmic plan to redeem the whole creation. Reformed theology teaches that we not only care about saving souls but also about restoring creation here and now. As such, we are passionate about evangelism, and we are passionate about redeeming the arts, education, business, social issues, politics, cities, science, and so on. All of creation belongs to Christ, and God's people are called to apply redemption to all things on earth as it is in heaven.

Reformed theology is then profoundly missional and enlists Jesus-followers to press the claims of Christ in every area of life as Christ currently sits on the throne as the reigning Davidic heir. Wolters correctly reminds us that "salvation in Jesus Christ conceived in the broad creational sense, means the restoration of culture and society in their present stage of development. . . . The coming Kingdom of God demands that these developments be reformed."[5] Namely, that culture and society are made answerable to their original design and are subjected to the desires of the Creator through the daily lives of the people of God.

We "preach the good news to all creation" (Mark 16:15, NIV) because the atonement deals with sin and evil permanently, but the scope of redemption also is "the recovery of creational goodness through the annulment of sin and the effort toward the progressive removal of its effects" as far as the curse is found.[6] Reformed theology is more than understanding that you are a sinner and cannot save yourself; it helps Jesus' followers see the full implications of the mission of the kingdom of God and the role of God's people in redemptive story.

The enemy of the church then is not "culture" but the work of the kingdom of Satan. Michael Williams concludes, "The goal of God's redemptive action in Jesus Christ is the destruction of the kingdom of Satan, sin and death, and the removal of the effects of sin upon man and creation."[7]

As a Reformed Christian, I stand in a long tradition of faithful followers of Christ who understand that living in the redemptive story here and now means that there is much work for Christians to do in the world. Out of my worship comes adoration and sending—praising the Lord that he has saved me by his grace through faith and that I have become a member of the people of God who are his workmanship, created in Christ Jesus to do good works, which God prepared in advance for us to do (Eph. 2:8–10). I realize that I am not simply saved *from* something (eternal punishment), but I am also saved *to* something: an eternity united to Jesus and a commission to follow him here and now. What a privilege! *Soli Deo gloria.*

4

Doesn't Everyone Believe the Same Thing?

ANTHONY J. CARTER

When I entered Bible college, I was as theologically green as a zealous young wanna-be preacher and theologian could be. Yet, it was not long before I realized that practically everyone in Bible college was as green as I was. And a large percentage of the students did not care to change. For most of them it was their first time away from home. And though they were in the sanitized environment of a Bible college, they nonetheless were out from under the watchful eye of Dad and Mom. For many it was more college than Bible. However, for me (and a handful of others) it was different.

From a Christless Christianity

I came to Atlanta Christian College from a life of Christless Christianity. I had never seen my father in church a day in my life; he died when I was ten years old. My mother, on the other hand, seemed to spend every free moment at church. Consequently, so did I. Professing faith at an early age was the folk religion of African-Americans in rural Michigan, and I was a *bona fide* convert to it. I don't recall how old I was when I stood before the church and said, "I believe in Jesus," but you can best believe I did—just as every one of my peers had done.

Church on Sunday was the obvious and obligatory destination of all children in my mother's house. When I finally left her house for college in 1985, I was no longer obliged to attend, and I didn't. Out from under the constraints of parental oversight, the Christlessness of my profession was exposed. And though I found myself in church from time to time, the effort was never anything more than a polite nod to my upbringing. Life outside of those infrequent church visits was licentious, hedonistic, and empty.

It was not until I moved to Atlanta in 1990 that I realized how empty my secular hedonism was. During my first year in Atlanta God arrested and changed my libertine heart, opened my eyes, and put Christ into my Christianity. Suddenly, the boy who could not wait to get away from church found himself wanting to be in church every day. This was the zealous yet naïve young man who arrived at Atlanta Christian College in January of 1992.

When I entered Atlanta Christian College, I was a nontraditional student. This was my second attempt at college. And this time, without the academically crippling distractions of athletic popularity, I was more focused on the task of education in general and of theological enlightenment in particular. I entered Bible college naïvely believing that everyone was zealous and had the same objectives. In fact, I believed that everyone believed the same thing. Man, was I wrong.

Doesn't Everyone Believe the Same Thing?

Believe it or not, I found Atlanta Christian College by way of the telephone book. Having recently come to a true experience of Jesus Christ and having had my world turned on its head by a Savior whom I saw as worthy of all my life (1 Tim. 1:12–17), I decided to reenter college with the purpose of getting a Bible education. As I searched around Atlanta for a Bible college, I looked for one that was fully accredited. I had dreams of attending seminary and did not want any complications due to my undergraduate institution. Atlanta Christian College (ACC) was the only fully accredited Bible College in the Atlanta area at the time. It was a no-brainer, so I thought. I took no serious thought concerning doctrine or practice, so long as it said Christian, taught from the Bible, and was accredited. After all, I was operating under the assumption that everyone believed the same thing. It was not long before it became apparent that I was woefully mistaken.

ACC is a college founded by, supported through, and affiliated with the Christian Churches and Churches of Christ. Though at the time I had no inclination what these were, I soon became aware of their history and doctrine. And when I was brought face to face with their teachings, clashes and discussions erupted in and out of class that significantly contributed to the man I would become. One such incident continues to stand out in my mind.

As a first-year student, I was required to take Christian Doctrine. One of the most respected and elder statesmen of this group of churches taught this particular class. In fact, he was the author of the two primary textbooks we used. It was clear that this man believed what he taught and had the courage of his convictions. He was just my type of teacher. Unfortunately, it became clear that we did not agree on our convictions, and one day in class everyone else learned that we did not agree as well.

As you might expect, the class discussion came to the all-important question, "What must a person do to be saved?" The position of the school and the professor was clear. Besides the evangelical understandings of faith in Christ and repentance from sin, the professor asserted the necessity of baptism by immersion. According to our textbook the reasons for baptism were:

1. In order to be saved (Mark 16:16).
2. For the remission (forgiveness) of sins (Acts 2:38).
3. For the washing away of sin (Acts 22:16).
4. For baptism into Christ (Rom. 6:3).[1]

Anyone familiar with the Christian Church or Churches of Christ would know their convictions concerning the necessity of baptism. Yet, I was far removed from knowing such difference of opinion among those who called themselves Christian.

As the professor made these points, and as the vast majority of the class nodded in agreement, I had the naïve and ignorant audacity to raise my hand in objection. I could sense the class coming to a halt, and before I knew it I said, "Sir, if baptism were necessary for salvation, then we would expect to see baptism in every salvation occurrence in Scripture. But we do not see that, do we?" When the professor began offering his rebuttal, I realized that not everyone believes the same thing. In fact, I began to realize that my view was the decidedly minority view.

The professor confidently assured the class that the conditions he had set forth for salvation were biblical. Then he turned his attention to me and squarely asked, "If a man professed faith in Christ on his dying bed and had no opportunity for baptism, would you give him the assurance of his salvation?" Again, the overly zealous and green Bible student spoke quickly, "Of course!" I blurted, "If I believed his confession to be sincere, then yes."

The aging professor answered with authority and voice raised, "You can't play God! This man would have lived his entire life in disobedience to God and now you would want to give him the assurance of faith on his death bed. No. I would tell him that his salvation is in God's hands and leave it at that." By now, there was a hush in the room as the elderly gentleman made it clear that no non-Christian church student was going to upstage him in the classroom. It became clear that some sense of normalcy was going to be difficult to reestablish. Fortunately, the clock struck lunchtime, and we all know that nothing says "normal" like lunchtime on a college campus. Out the doors we went.

However, if I thought it was over, I was sorely mistaken. By the time I reached the cafeteria, word of the exchange had already reached the servers, and whispers could be heard throughout the place. "Did you hear that guy speaking to the professor like that?" Another said, "I'm glad someone finally said something."

Still others quietly commented using words like "disrespectful" and "out of line." This was new and strange territory for me. The exchange began to make my reputation around campus as a theological thinker. But I still was not clear on what my own thinking was. I began to be more conscious of theological differences and became more intent on knowing what I believed and why. And it was not long after this incident that the Lord began to show me the faith that my heart professed. I discovered it in the oddest of places doing the most menial of tasks.

A Day of Discovery

A proud young Bible college student is not much interested in the menial task of clearing Sunday school material out of a storage room. Yet this was my responsibility in the winter of 1994. The room was filled with outdated material. There were half-completed Sunday school lessons, teacher's guides, overhead transparencies (remember those?), and piles and piles of Bible study books on just about every Bible theme. And there were some videotapes.

As I made my way through the material, a single videotape caught my attention. The case was dark blue with red lettering with the design of a cross on the front. The title on the tape case was *The Cross of Christ*, and the name on the case was R. C. Sproul. I had come across this Sproul guy during some of my readings, but had never seen him or listened to him. Yet, since I was into this cross thing and this Christ thing, I thought it would be a good idea to at least watch the tape before I threw it away. The video was actually part of a two-set video series. The first tape was missing; the second part to the series was all I had. Little did I know that the second part was all that I would need.

As I watched and listened to the stout, engaging, Pennsylvanian-accented white man, I was riveted to the television screen. He spoke of justification by faith in a way that I had never heard. His illustrations were vivid, his enthusiasm infectious, and his theological insights and understanding impressive, to say the least. He spoke of the great exchange and how in justification my sins were imputed to Christ and Christ's righteousness was imputed to me. I had read books on justification and had heard preachers preach and teachers teach on justification. Yet, for the first time this wonderful, indispensable doctrine was made real to me, and I understood it. What God had done for me in Christ overwhelmed my soul. I did not know who this R. C. Sproul was, but I knew I believed what he believed. To this day, *The Cross of Christ* remains my favorite video series from R.C. Sproul. It was my first, but it surely would not be my last.

After watching the video, I called a couple of my closest friends and told them that they had to see R. C. Sproul. Later that evening we watched the video together. It was not long before we were ordering other video tapes: *The Holiness of God*, *Chosen by God*, *The Providence of God*, *Romans*, and many others. Before long, books by R. C. Sproul became a staple in our diet of reading. We not only read books by Sproul, but also books he referenced or recommended. I soon became aware that the Reformed theology I had embraced by default was the Reformed theology I was now embracing with all intent. I was learning as much theology out of class as I was learning in class. Soon it began to show.

Back at Atlanta Christian College, I had gained the reputation as the campus Calvinist. I recall that a certain church history professor, a rather gentle, amicable, humorous, and self-deprecating, yet most capable man, was teaching on the Reformation. One day the subject was the five points of Calvinism. As he wrote the letters for the acrostic TULIP on the board, he asked the class for the specific doctrine associated with each letter. Some one blurted out, "Total depravity." I was quietly encouraged by the accuracy. However, it was short-lived. Someone in the back said, "Unlimited atonement." Another said boldly, "Unconditional grace." Before it could get any worse, I offered, "Unconditional election." The professor acknowledged my affinity for Calvinism and asked if I would do everyone the favor of listing the other three. I gladly said, "Limited atonement, irresistible grace, and the perseverance of the saints." The campus Calvinist had spoken. There was no going back.

The remaining time of my Bible college tenure provided many opportunities for me to become more firm in what I believed and ready to give an answer for the hope within me. I have learned to appreciate my time at Atlanta Christian College, because I had to study more diligently in order to stand up for what I believed to be the truth. The professor and students who disagreed with me, for the most part, did so with grace and love. While I did not share some of their theological convictions, I did find good friends among the faculty and students. I also found that if you ever want to know how well you understand something, spend extended time among those who don't agree with you. It will break you of your belief, or make you all the more firm in it. Thankfully, for me it was the latter.

As graduation approached, one of my professors approached me and asked if I was interested in going to seminary. I told him, "Yes, I am." He asked if I would be interested in attending one of the seminaries associated with the college. I deeply appreciated his interest in me. It showed that as a man of faith, he could look beyond our obvious disagreements and see that I was, like him, serious about the ministry and training for it. He sincerely desired to see me in seminary and particularly in a seminary closely associated with his church. I took this as a compliment and thanked him for his interest in me. However, I informed him that I had been long enough in an environment where my views and convictions were ever challenged. I wanted to go where I could find theological affinity with fellow students and professors. When I did attend seminary, it was a welcomed respite to listen and learn in an environment that was not antagonistic to my growing love for Reformed theology. Reformed Theological Seminary (RTS) proved to be just the place.

Orlando or Bust

The decision to go to seminary was not a question of "if" but "where." I quickly narrowed my decision to two choices: Reformed Theological Seminary in Orlando or Trinity Evangelical Divinity School in Deerfield, Illinois. A visit to Orlando's campus in the balmy month of February sealed the deal. While most people probably think that the choice of seminary is a much prayed over and soul-examining decision, for me it was basically a decision of whether I wanted to be in Chicago in January and February or Orlando. Besides, R. C. Sproul was in Orlando. I did not need any more persuading.

Going to seminary was one of the best moves I have ever made. No doubt, it was an often difficult training ground. The work was heavy. Family life was demanding. And of course, money was tight. Yet, those years were some of the best, as I really fell in love with my wife even as we matured as disciples of Christ and as parents. Though the seminary years were difficult and taxing, I would not trade them for anything. More than the Bible (and I did learn much about the Bible), seminary taught me about me. And man, those were some important lessons. In fact, one lesson in particular continues to stand out as an epochal moment in my Reformed theological journey. And I have Richard Pratt to thank for it.

It Would Never Be the Same

When I entered seminary, my thinking and practices were being greatly influenced by some of the more popular evangelical and Reformed preachers of the day. I listened regularly to men like R. C. Sproul, John MacArthur, Steve Brown, James Montgomery Boice, Chuck Swindoll, and Ravi Zacharias. These men had regular radio preaching ministries from which I gleaned much of my approach to ministry and preaching. They were my contemporary heroes (with John Newton and D. Martyn Lloyd-Jones being my deceased heroes). I wanted to be like them. I wanted to preach like them, if that were possible. Their preaching and teaching shaped my thinking and the attitude I had toward me and my gifts. This was true until I walked into Reformed Theological Seminary's mandatory first-year class taught by Dr. Richard Pratt. Nothing would ever be the same.

During my pre-enrollment visit in February 1996, I learned that R. C. Sproul had recently resigned his professorship at RTS

Orlando. As you can imagine, this was a hard pill for me to swallow. My host assured me that while Sproul would be missed, I would find Richard Pratt the teacher of choice around the seminary. I quickly learned how true his words were.

Pratt was the most popular professor on campus. Many students found his sometimes over-the-top approach refreshing and genuine, while others were turned off by it. He was rarely without controversy. He was unexpected, sharp, incomparably intelligent, witty, tall, and sometimes even awkward. He spoke of taking dancing lessons with his wife, but when I watched him walk, I could only imagine the pain and agony of his wife and instructor. He was a geek in a full beard, and yet you just got the sincere feeling that he desired to know you and relate to you.

However, he was also edgy, and when those edges got close to you and your worldview, they would cut. Suddenly, the professor you thought was your friend could become an antagonist as he deconstructed your notions of yourself and what you perceived to be true. One day he caught me off guard: he began to speak unflatteringly about some popular evangelical preachers who left no room for what he called "fuzzy areas." In other words, they spoke and preached as if they were the keepers of biblical truth because they had so wonderfully and faithfully handled the history and grammar of New Testament Greek. Accordingly, when antecedents are properly identified and verbs rightly conjugated, the truth of the New Testament is always clearly known. Richard constantly warned us not to drink the Kool-Aid.

This was not the first time Pratt had spoken in this negative tone concerning many of the men I considered heroes. Yet, for some reason that day I had had enough. After class, I asked if I could have a word with him. I was seriously considering dropping the class. He graciously agreed to talk to me. My first question was, "Do you believe everything you say, or is it just for effect?" He smiled and replied, "Yes. I believe what I teach and much of it is for effect."

He went on to explain to me that most of the men in the class were white, middle- to upper-middle-class southern Presbyterians. They had a view of the world that was skewed by their dominant cultural perspective. Yet, they were going to be sent to minister the gospel in a world where the vast majority of people was radically different than they were. Richard saw that his task was to shake them out of their skewed perspective and presumption, and hopefully open them up to ministry outside of themselves.

My next question was, "Well, what about me?"

Richard looked straight at me as we stood in the courtyard of RTS and spoke the words I will never forget: "The Holy Spirit wants to use the experiences God has given you to speak the truths of his Word through you." When he spoke those words, I thought how God desired to use me as a black man to proclaim the truths of his Word. It dawned on me that God did not desire for me to become "white" or even to preach like James Boice or R. C. Sproul. Rather, God would take biblical Reformed theology and teach me to be me. My contributions to the kingdom of God would be not in how much I could become like my white heroes, but in yielding to the Holy Spirit and allowing him to use this black man to proclaim his truth. Studying, preaching, and teaching Reformed theology would never be the same for me.

From then on, Pratt became my favorite teacher. Often I would chuckle inside as some fellow student would experience one of Richard's edges in class, and the student would be left wondering if he was really called to gospel ministry. By the end of the course that same student would join with every other student in giving Richard a standing round of applause for another course well taught—and for reassuring us that our confidence must not be in our culture, experiences, or even heroes. We must put our confidence and assurance in God and the Bible, his inerrant self-revelation.

Richard taught me to be Reformed, yet always be reforming (*semper reformanda*). I have never looked back. Today I am the living legacy of men like Augustine and John Calvin, John Bunyan and D. Martyn Lloyd-Jones. But also, and as far as I am concerned, even more gloriously, I am the living legacy of men like Olaudah Equiano and Lemuel Haynes, Francis Grimke and Daniel Payne, Carl Ellis and Ken Jones. Today I am an African-

American who embraces the biblical theology commonly known as Reformed theology. I rejoice to know that I am not the first to do so, and by God's grace, I will not be the last.

What Difference Has Reformed Theology Made?

I will be the first to admit that I am not the sharpest tool in God's toolbox. Therefore, one of the important elements of my Christian experience has been the necessity of historical connections. In other words, I am always looking for men and women who have believed what I believe. I am not interested in being out on the theological island by myself without the help and confirming camaraderie of those who have gone before. One of the glories of biblical Reformed theology is that it is historical. We have the awesome blessing of knowing that there have been and continue to be others who confess the very same thing we confess today. True Christianity is never a faith in isolation. Our faith must be a continuous line of faithful men and women who testify to the faithfulness of God and give proof that our God has never been without a witness among the people of the earth. The Reformed tradition gives me confidence that I am indeed a part of that continuous line.

Reformed theology reminds us that we are connected. The great Reformed confessions and catechisms, along with the historical creeds, provide for us a theological and practical link to those who have gone before us.[2] When we read these confessions and recite these catechisms, we are reading and reciting the same biblical faith of saints centuries removed from us.

This allows and even encourages our connection with the saints of God who have been made perfect as they have gone on to their eternal bliss in the presence of Christ. The writer of Hebrews reminds us that New Testament worship is a truly multi-generational and celestial worship. Whenever we gather, we join in worship with the angels; the church triumphant is made up of the spirits of the righteous saints who have been make perfect and are in the presence of Jesus Christ, whose precious blood has made this worship possible (Heb. 12:18–28). The historical connections of Reformed theology have given me a sense that I am not alone in my faith. And thus, it has also made me a more intentional, thoughtful, and emotional worshiper.

Reformed theology continues to make me a better worshiper by giving me a bigger, more glorious picture of God and a more accurate assessment of myself. John Calvin begins his *Institutes of the Christian Religion* with these essential points: "Without knowledge of self there is no knowledge of God," and "without knowledge of God there is no knowledge of self."[3] It could be argued that the *Institutes* is essentially John Calvin's unfolding of the biblical theology of the knowledge of God and the knowledge of humanity. True knowledge leads to a displeasure with oneself and ultimately to a desire for the pleasure and intimacy of God. Reformed theology has helped me to better grasp both of these truths.

For example, the doctrine of total depravity is a foundational truth of the Scriptures and thus of Reformed theology.[4] At first, even the sound of the words "total" and "depravity" can seem so final and irredemiably bad because we believe that so few people, if any, are beyond reform. Yet, it was not until I came to grips with the depths of my own sinfulness that I really began to understand the glories of God's grace. Great sinners require greater grace supplied by an even greater Savior.

The Bible and Reformed theology exalt grace so much because sin is so awful. When the Bible says, "Where sin increased, grace abounded all the more" (Rom. 5:20), Reformed theology says, "Yes!" Thus, in response, the worship I experience is a worship seeking less of me and more of grace. The worship I experience is a worship that exults in the gospel of Jesus because I stand so in need of it. It is reflective of a boast and a glory in the cross and not me (Gal. 6:14). In other words, the worship I experience is a worship of a heart filled with the truth of Reformed theology, like that of John Newton.

It is no surprise that the most beloved hymn in all of Christianity was written by a confessing Reformed theology preacher. As a friend of mine is fond of reminding me that only a Reformed theologian could have written:

Amazing Grace, how sweet the sound;
That saved a wretch like me.
I once was lost, but now am found;
Was blind but now I see.

Every day of my life, my worship flows from the growing reality of my sinfulness and the ever-increasing glory of God's sovereign grace in the person and work of Jesus Christ on my behalf.

John Newton's eyesight was almost gone by the end of his life. He would enter his pulpit for only a few moments, and say, "I am a great sinner, but I have a great Savior." Reformed theology teaches us to echo the sentiments of Newton, and, as a wonderful consequence, makes us better fit for the worship of God.

5

Grace and Greater Union

KEN JONES

Since this volume consists of essays by African-American Christians explaining their journeys into the doctrines of grace, I want to begin by expressing my great surprise when I came to know these doctrines. I was surprised at how rare it is to be an African-American Christian who consciously and intentionally embraces reformational theology. We are as rare as black Republicans (and probably viewed with as much suspicion as those "sell-out" blacks who have the nerve to break rank with traditional black political alliances) and are viewed as oddballs in the religious sector of the black community. It is our rarity that makes this volume an interesting project.

The first Reformed conference I attended was in San Diego in 1991. Of the fifteen hundred people in attendance, I was one of an estimated ten or twenty blacks. While this did get my attention, I was neither bothered nor put off by it. However, my presence did get the attention of some of the conference organizers, one of whom made it a point to come over and speak to me during the breaks. The more we talked, the more it became apparent that this brother had a threefold curiosity: (1) What brought me, an African-American Christian, to this Reformed event? (2) Did I have any thoughts on why more African-Americans were not in attendance? (3) Did I have any suggestions on how to attract more African-Americans to such events? It's been almost twenty years since that conference, and since then I have attended and spoken at numerous Reformed conferences. For the most part the presence of African-American Christians, at best, has been scarce. And in one form or another I am repeatedly asked how I came to the doctrines of grace. In fact, when I encounter other blacks at these gatherings, I usually put the same question to them. So, as uncomfortable as it is for me to talk about myself, here is the story of my journey.

I was raised in a traditional, conservative National Baptist Convention church. From an early age church was enjoyable to me. I took great pleasure in worship, BTU (Baptist Training Union), Junior Mission, and Junior Laymen programs. In addition I had a next-door neighbor who was the only black member of a Nazarene church. This lady was a bundle of energy that was mostly directed at child evangelism. I was a member of the Good News Club she hosted in her home. Eventually I attended Sunday school at her church and became part of the LTL (Loyal Temperance Legion), which was an organization geared toward teaching children about the evils of alcohol. Through the combined activities in my home church and involvement with my next-door neighbor (which also involved summer camp with the LTL), I learned the books of the Bible and memorized Scripture. I learned the Lord's Prayer and the Ten Commandments, and I came to realize that I was a sinner and that Jesus died for sinners. I did not "accept Jesus as my personal Savior" until I was twelve years old, but I had read through the Bible twice by then. I cannot stress enough even to this day my overwhelming gratitude for my Sunday school teachers, and especially my neighbor, Mrs. Johnson, for their diligence in teaching the Bible to a child with perhaps an unusual hunger for the Word of God.

My experience as a member of a traditional black Baptist church while simultaneously being involved with a white evangelical church would prove to be invaluable in later years as I became more cognizant of theological issues. Even at an early age I noticed a difference in the worship of the two congregations. The Nazarene church seemed to be more intentional and consistent in teaching their "holiness" doctrine. It should also be noted that my home church was located in the heart of Watts, California, which erupted in severe rioting in 1965, the year I turned seven. The Nazarene church was located in Compton, a few miles south of Watts. While at that time more minorities were moving into Compton, the political leadership was white, as were most of the churches. Ironically, in 1970 my home church would purchase the building owned by the Nazarene church because most of the Nazarene church members had moved away from the city.

The riots of 1965 revealed another striking difference between the two churches. In my home church in Watts I clearly remember hearing our pastor raise issues about social justice, even as he admonished the congregation not to be seduced into thinking this uprising was a viable response to injustice. Driving to church down 103rd Street was like going through a war zone with armed National Guard members at every major intersection and familiar businesses smoldering in ashes. I can't say I remember much more about the preaching at the Nazarene church during that period, but there was a noticeable falloff in attendance. I do, however, recall Mrs. Johnson's nephew, who was a few years older than me, teasing her about how "these white folks were afraid of her now." As I think back on that period, it must have been far more traumatic than I could even imagine for Mrs. Johnson and the Nazarene congregation, not to mention extremely awkward as she and they dealt with the fear and unspoken questions stirred by the situation.

It was these two churches that shaped my early understanding of the Christian faith. The turbulent '60s, ripe with racial tensions, was the backdrop against which the shaping took place. Hindsight is indeed twenty-twenty, and as I look back I now understand that for the most part, and for all of their external differences (race, denomination, style of worship, and methodology), the two churches were very similar in their depiction of the Christian faith and life. Both churches emphasized the fact that Jesus died for our sins and that one needed to accept him as one's personal Savior. And both defined the Christian life in moralistic terms.

My family had strong ties to our small Baptist church in the heart of Watts. Once when my mother was sick, I came home from school to find women from the church doing our laundry and cooking our meals. Later when my mother was hospitalized, my sisters and I stayed with different church members until an aunt came from Arkansas to stay with us while my father worked two jobs. I mention all of this to emphasize what I stated above: I am extremely grateful to God for the people he placed in my life during those formative years. Truly, ours was a church where there was genuine and tangible love.

Although I had yet to profess faith in Jesus as "my personal Savior" (largely because I was far too shy to come forward during the invitation that followed every sermon), I truly loved the Lord and tried to live in a manner that was pleasing to him. I absolutely loved listening to preaching and would go with my father to revival meetings throughout the city to hear well-known preachers from around the country when they came to town. On Sunday evenings we would also go to worship services that were broadcast live on the radio. These sermons were always arousing and uplifting. It didn't take long to pick up on the clichés and catchphrases that seemed to punctuate most of the sermons I heard. In the preaching that I was exposed to, style was the key. It wasn't just a matter of what the preacher said, but how he said it. Genuine black preaching was punctuated with the "whoop," the sing-song intonations that provoked verbal response from the congregation. Given my fondness for listening to sermons, it seems fitting that my introduction to Reformed theology would come through a sermon. However, it was not a sermon that I *heard*, but rather one that I read in a high school literature class: Jonathan Edwards's "Sinners in the Hands of an Angry God."

My Own Awakening

The purpose of the literature class assignment was to present New England Puritanism in a negative light. Yet, I was mesmerized from the outset, realizing that this sermon was like no other sermon I had ever heard. Edwards's text for the sermon was Deuteronomy 32:35: "Their foot shall slide in due time" (KJV). Two things caught my attention immediately. First, in the introduction, Edwards stated that the Israelites to whom the text was addressed "lived under the means of grace." The expression "means of grace" was unfamiliar to me, but from my dispensational upbringing I assumed that Israel was under the law and not grace (which according to my understanding was not available until the coming of Christ). This may not have been an accurate account of what my church taught, but it is what I understood to be the gist of what was taught. Second, Edwards's depiction of the sovereign justice of God also caught my attention. I previously had heard sermons on hell that could probably be described as fire-and-brimstone; but I had heard nothing like this.

Reading this sermon led me to libraries and bookstores for other works by Edwards. Biographical notes spoke of his stern Calvinism and his opposition to Arminianism; both terms were new to me, and even as I researched them they didn't fully register. My research, however, led to other preachers, namely George Whitefield and Charles Spurgeon. The sermons of these men and Edwards exposed me to completely different preaching than I was accustomed to. These sermons were Christ-centered and were more than mere moral exhortations to do better and to keep "trusting the Lord" in spite of the storms of life. Yet, as helpful as those sermons were, my spiritual life was still a mess as I struggled with assurance and sin even though I was active in my church.

From high school through college I tried every remedy that was offered to cure my spiritual schizophrenia—from re-dedication, to fasting, to heartfelt promises to try harder. I even gave away my secular music collection. Yet, the three things that accelerated my journey toward the doctrines of grace were a professor in the religion department of my university, J. I. Packer's *Knowing God*, and Stephen Charnock's *The Existence and Attributes of God*.

I had the religion professor for two classes: Introduction to the Bible and Jesus the Christ. He made it clear on the first day of class in Introduction to the Bible that the Scofield Study Bible was unwelcome in his class. Because I had a brand new Scofield (and was proud of it), I went to his office later in the week to find out what his issue was. Among other things, he informed me that without my trusty Scofield Bible and particularly its footnotes, I would not be as versed as I was on the seven dispensations. This was the first time that the dispensationalism in which I had grown up was ever challenged. But, it was really in the Jesus the Christ class that things began to click. For the first time the office of Messiah was expounded in more detail than I had ever heard before. The course did not strongly emphasize the concept of covenant, but I learned enough about it to gain a better understanding of what it meant when I claimed that "Jesus died for my sins."

I spent much time in this rebel Church of Christ minister/professor's office, and it was evident to him that I didn't understand what it meant to be a Protestant. Surprisingly (as I look back on it now), he recommended that I read Calvin's *Institutes of the Christian Religion*. I didn't read this work all the way through initially, but what I did read helped me to get a better handle on the assurance of salvation. More importantly I was introduced to the doctrine of justification. From there three things began to happen. First, I began to see my salvation in a more christocentric light. I now understood that Jesus not only died for my sins, but he also lived for my righteousness. Second, I began to understand the importance of doctrine. Up to this point I had bought into the idea that doctrine divides and that Christianity is about relationships. But reading Calvin's *Institutes* helped me to understand that doctrine does not undermine the relational aspect of Christianity, rather it defines and undergirds it. Third, reading *The Institutes* enabled me to appreciate the importance of apologetics, the defense of the faith. *The Institutes*, combined with Charnock and Packer, provided much needed depth and breadth to my faith. I wouldn't say that I was fully Reformed at this point, but I had a better understanding of my salvation, and assurance was no longer a problem.

My First Reformed Conference

In 1983 I was called to pastor a church plant in Carson, California. Within one year we relocated to North Long Beach, which borders the city of Compton. I served that congregation for six years before being called to the church where I presently serve. During those six years I would describe my preaching as more doctrinal and Christ-centered than the preaching I had grown up with, but with hints of moralism and Jesus as example still present.

My first two years at Greater Union Baptist Church were pivotal in shaping my eventual full embrace of Reformed theology. The critical ingredient that began to bring everything together was a Ligonier conference in San Diego. I had read R. C. Sproul's *Chosen by God,* so I looked forward to hearing him speak. But what really drew me to the conference was the opportunity to hear J. I. Packer, who had written *Knowing God.* The theme of the conference was "The Majesty of Christ." That conference was as close to an epiphany as I have ever experienced. All of my patchwork understanding of Reformed theology finally found a place where it could be refined and fine-tuned. I was enriched by all the speakers as well as by conversing with others in attendance during the breaks. And the bookstore: Wow! Not only did I purchase books to take home, but I read almost entire chapters of others while standing in the bookstore.

Attending that first Ligonier conference was an experience of such value and spiritual enlightenment that trying to explain it would be an injustice. For the first time I was hearing the doctrines that had consumed me for years expounded upon with clarity and biblical and theological integrity. God's glory became the grid through which I began to see all of salvation. I now understood that the person and work of Christ is the culmination of the divine glory. And grace became for me the riches, the splendor, the unspeakable joy, and refulgence of Scripture. I became a new pastor at that conference. Hearing all of those expositions of God's glory was like a magnificent light shining on my religious world and experience, exposing the shallowness, the emotionalism, the busywork, the man-centeredness, the false confidence, and the pride that had previously eclipsed the glory of the Triune God. My journey up to this point had convinced me that my religious upbringing was flawed at best, but now I could see just how flawed it was. The brand of evangelicalism I had been exposed to had drifted from historical Protestantism by replacing grace with an unhealthy blend of human effort and divine assistance. The Christian life depicted in this system was a religious version of the American dream. But more specifically I realized that the "black church" (I don't mean just the local church in which I grew up, but that entity called the "black church" defined by social and emotional elements that transcend denomination and geography) was a system within the system of a flawed evangelicalism.

The reason I say I became a new pastor is because that conference, coupled with what I had been grappling with over the years, sparked within me a passion to bring the glory of God manifested in the doctrines of grace to bear on the black church, at least in that portion of the vineyard in which I served.

Gospel Friendships

Before I go further in discussing my efforts to implement the doctrines of grace into the life of Greater Union Baptist Church, I must mention something else that came as a result of Ligonier Ministries. In the spring of 1992 I was invited by a Ligonier staff person to attend a luncheon to promote the full conference later that year. The speaker was Michael Horton, a young author and president of Christians United for Reformation (CURE). I was familiar with Horton's book, *The Agony of Deceit,* and the person who invited me thought it would be good for Michael and me to meet. We became brothers at first sight. His organization was committed to bringing reformation to all of evangelicalism; I was trying to reform a black church.

As Michael and I spent time together, I was eventually drafted into the ranks and service of CURE, teaching doctrine and church history Friday nights at the Academy (Lynwood CURE Academy was established by CURE to train pastors and lay leaders in Bible and theology in the Compton and Lynwood areas). I would also, on occasion, co-host the fledgling radio program, *The White Horse Inn*. Eventually, I was appointed dean of the Lynwood CURE Academy and became a regular co-host on *The White Horse Inn*, along with Michael, Kim Riddlebarger, and Rod Rosenbladt. I mention this association because Mike, Kim, and Rod have been gracious and committed teachers as well as trusted friends. They have no idea (although I have tried to express it to them) how much they helped me connect the dots of reformational theology. Their prayers, conversations, and insights—along with their listening ears—have been as much a part of the reforming work that has taken place at Greater Union as has been my teaching. They recognize that the theological afflictions of the evangelical system are the same across the board, regardless of ethnicity or culture. But at the same time they realize that ethnicity and culture create different contexts in which these afflictions are played out, and consequently there are different challenges to overcome. Their support and sensitivity as I have labored in the unique context of the "black church" and their patience as I have addressed issues relative to that unique setting (of which they have no point of reference) is greatly appreciated.

Grace and Greater Union

So, how did Reformed theology come to a traditional black church like Greater Union? Let me explain a little about the church before discussing the transformation. At the time I was elected pastor, the church had just gone through a split. It had about 125 members with at least 150–175 people who would attend each week. Within the first year of my pastorate both of those numbers increased. In some respects Greater Union was

typical of most black Baptist churches in that there was a dispro-
portionate number of women members on the membership role
and in attendance. Gospel choir music, as opposed to congregational singing, was a central part of the worship. The atmosphere
of the worship service was highly charged and emotional. There
were a host of activities to give people something to do. And
there were the annual days common to most black churches (i.e.
Youth Day, Usher's Day, Women's Day, Men's Day, etc.). Those
days consisted of Sunday afternoon worship services with one or
more guest churches (with their choirs) in attendance, a specific
theme, a talk on that theme, and a sermon by a guest pastor. In
addition to having our own annual days, we were often invited
to be the guests for annual days at other churches. Also typical
of most black churches is that midweek prayer meeting and Bible
study were poorly attended. What I have described was not much
different from what I had grown up with in my home church;
the exception was that worship services at Greater Union were
more consistently fervent and emotionally charged. But for all
of the things that were typical of black Baptist churches shared
by Greater Union, there were also some significant differences.
Some spoke in tongues, healing services apparently had been a
part of the church, some held to Word-Faith teachings, and the
members were accustomed to having joint worship services with
Pentecostal churches.

These charismatic elements in a Baptist setting are pretty
much commonplace today. But in the early '90s it was somewhat rare, because Baptists were still Baptist whether Arminian or Calvinistic. So in some respects Greater Union was on
the cutting edge of the changing face of evangelicalism. It was
against this backdrop of a traditional black church with charismatic and Word-Faith leanings that I endeavored to establish a
new theological foundation. In the balance of this chapter I will
outline in broad terms the steps taken to bring about change.
I say in broad terms, because it is not my intention to go into
all of the details of the changes or the resistance and resultant
fallout.

Reformed Preaching/Teaching

As previously stated, by the time I came to Greater Union, my preaching had already undergone significant change. With the pieces of reformational theology coming together, I became even more Christ-centered in my preaching and much more doctrinal. But it wasn't just the content of the preaching that changed; it was also the style and manner in which the messages were delivered. I was never a "whooper" in the classic sense of traditional black preaching. But I knew how to work up my audience with a certain flair, turn of a phrase, gesture, "rhetorical runs," and exuberant exhortations. And some of these elements are still present in my preaching. Perhaps what is behind this style of preaching is the unspoken notion that what validated a sermon was the emotional and verbal response of the people. In most black worship services that I attended, a sermon met with silence indicated one of two things: either the congregation was "dead" and didn't know how to "get with" the preacher, or the sermon itself was a dud. In either case the preacher's goal was to move the people or (in preacher slang) to "slay the house." It's not that content wasn't important, because it was. One had to know the right clichés and phrases to use in order to move people. But the content that moved people was not the glory of God as seen in the person and work of Christ—at least in most cases. While attending Ligonier conferences I realized I was greatly moved by the messages I heard. What moved me was not the delivery, but rather the content those men were declaring. I detected no conscious effort on the part of the speakers to arouse their hearers (if that was their intent, I did not see it). They simply expounded the Scripture, and I was enriched by their commitment to do so.

Consequently, the change in my preaching began with a different aim. My aim was no longer to move the people, but rather to open the Word of God and expound the person and work of Christ. I intentionally toned down my passion and rhetorical skills. I no longer saw the need to be motivational or to be a cheerleader. It became clear to me that the tradition that I had been reared in had, intentionally or not, confused the power and presence of the Spirit with human emotions. It's not that I personally disapproved of the amens and other responses, but I no longer evaluated my sermons by those responses. Now, I wanted the gospel to be clear and Christ to be uppermost. Paul's words in 1 Corinthians 2:1–5 became my aim in preaching. It took time to break some old habits, but I made a conscious commitment to consistently and clearly preach Christ. Understandably, in the words of some, I was no longer a dynamic preacher but more a teacher and lecturer.

In conjunction with this commitment to preach Christ clearly and consistently, I devoted my Bible studies to a systematic teaching of the doctrines of the faith. This meant exhaustive expositions of whole books of the Bible and in-depth studies of specific doctrines like justification, the atonement, and election. As I interacted with the membership of Greater Union, I began to see that while many were avid Bible readers and were familiar with passages and biblical language, they did not know the basic doctrines of the faith. Wednesday nights and Sunday school were devoted to doctrinal studies. My point was that it is not enough to say that the Bible is the Word of God; we must know what that Word says and what it means. Knowing what the Word says and means serves to build us up in the knowledge of Christ, and it provides protection from erroneous doctrine.

Come Inside

Part of my extensive teaching during this period included Protestant and Baptist history. My own background helped me understand the absence of any significant knowledge about the distinctives of the Baptist denomination or the different types of Baptist churches—not to mention knowledge about the sixteenth-century Reformation or significant church figures like Augustine, Luther, and Calvin. Therefore, I came to understand the important task of teaching church history on Wednesday nights. Part of my motivation was to get people to see that faith in Christ engrafts us into the whole of church history. Furthermore, I wanted them to realize that the "new doctrines" that I was teaching were not new but were in fact "the faith once delivered to all the saints." The reason these doctrines appeared new was because the church, the evangelical church (and the black church), had strayed from the apostles' doctrine and the parameters of Protestantism. I wanted them to step outside the box that is the black church and into the stream of historic Protestantism. With Sam Waldron's *Baptist Roots in America* as a guide I presented the distinctives of Particular (Calvinistic) Baptists and General (Arminian) Baptists and let them decide which one they thought was most consistent with Scripture. I also taught the great confessions of Protestantism, particularly the London Confession of 1689.

Teaching on church history proved to be most helpful in contextualizing the preaching that took place on Sundays. But in addition it was a delight to see members identifying themselves with the ranks of Protestantism. One brother distributed copies of the Westminster Confession, from which the 1689 Confession is drawn. One sister asked permission to make Luther's Smaller Catechism available at the church. Another sister read Luther's tract *Christian Liberty* with great benefit and shared it with others. Another sister, a college student, reported with glee that one of her Western Civilization courses was studying the Protestant Reformation. Because of what she had learned in church, she had a point of reference for that class. Many responded that they were now ready to participate in a conversation from which they had previously been excluded. Now they understood why they were Protestants and what type of Baptists they were. They now appreciated Presbyterians and Lutherans even as they understood our differences on key issues.

What about Worship?

The worship of the "black church" is probably the most obvious and overt expression of its distinctives. The music, the expressions of praise, the testimonies, and the atmosphere of excitement reach a culminating crescendo in the preaching moment. Let me be absolutely clear on this: it was not my intention, nor has it ever been, to prohibit the kind of emotional expressiveness characteristic of the black worship experience. I did intend, however, to consciously not promote emotionalism. We made significant changes to our order of service, changes that made the Word of God and the person and work of Christ central to the service. As a result, the tone of the services changed. Whatever the issues and arguments raised in the debate over worship style, worship of the triune God is to be reverent. And I was convinced that reverence had been lost or confused in the worship service at Greater Union. This is a very touchy subject with black churches, because for some, the emotional atmosphere of a black worship service authenticates our participation in what has been called "the white man's religion."

Be that as it may, I was more concerned with structuring a worship service that was not only God-centered but also consistent with his Word. God has always been the One who determines what is proper or improper, appropriate or inappropriate in the worship expressions of his covenant people. In fact worship is a divine mandate to the people of God to receive from him and to respond to his gracious acts. The biblical accounts of Cain's rejected sacrifice (Gen. 4:1–7), the golden calf fiasco (Ex. 32:1–35), and the strange fire offered by Nadab and Abihu (Num. 3:1–4) all illustrate that human innovation and sincerity are not the hallmarks of appropriate worship. We are to worship God as he has instructed in his Word. At Greater Union we began to emphasize corporate worship. In biblical worship, not only do we gather in a common place, but we lift our voices together in song, recite Scripture together in responsive readings, hear God's Word preached together, and give corporate prayer prominence.

Allow me to make two comments about music. (I will not comment on musical styles or the cultural assumptions within or about music in the black church.) The two things that concern me most are the content of the songs we sing and establishing congregational singing as a priority. As previously stated, preaching and teaching were the primary means of bringing the light of reformational theology to bear on our local church. As such, it was through teaching that we were able to demonstrate the importance of corporate singing in public worship. And it was also through teaching that we were able to call attention to the content of the songs that we sang. In fact, in one of our Bible studies I went through some of the hymns in our National Baptist Hymnal and pointed out what was good or bad about certain hymns. Furthermore I gave our musician a list of hymns approved for worship and indicated that all other songs that were to be introduced had to be approved first. Bible teaching provides the theology of worship, and songs old and new should be selected on the basis of their consistency with that theology.

Breaking Ties

As stated previously, joint worship services in celebration of various annual days is a big part of the black church experience. As the doctrines of grace began to occupy a more prominent place in the life of our church, many of our old fellowships and affiliations were broken. These broken fellowships can be explained by a number of reasons . For one thing, the invitations stopped coming. I can only speculate, but I think other churches were not comfortable with the changes they saw when they visited with us. In most cases the invitation system is reciprocal. For example, if a church invites you to a Men's Day service, you might in turn invite them to an Usher's Day service. As part of our reforming process we had eliminated all such annual days except for our church anniversary. I won't explain the rationale behind that decision, because to do so would take me too far afield from the subject at hand. But the churches we had longstanding fellowship with did not share our theological and doctrinal convictions. For a while we still invited some of these churches to our church anniversary services. Admittedly, this was a compromise on my part, because in extending the invitation I was allowing men to preach who might or might not get the gospel right. There is no excuse for such compromise, and looking back on it even now causes me to be ashamed. I think I was trying to prove to myself and to my critics that I had not abandoned the black church. By continuing to invite traditional black churches to our church anniversary, I was making the statement that although our doctrine is different, we are still connected. This was a mistake and a poor discharge of my duties as a pastor. What resulted were awkward joint worship services with hosts and guests recognizing that we were on completely different pages. This should never be the case in a Christian worship service. Furthermore, I had stopped accepting invitations to anything but church anniversary or mission day services, which made pastors reluctant to engage in any form of fellowship. In short, I could no longer in good conscience expose the flock, for which I have been given oversight, to practices and doctrine that did not line up with what we held and confessed.

Today we continue to invite churches to join in worship services with us during our church anniversary. However, we invite churches with which we share theological and doctrinal convictions. Unfortunately, most of these churches are not from the immediate area, and most are not black churches. This does not mean that we have turned our backs on the black church community. I personally have continued to maintain contact with some local black pastors as well as some outside of the area. But for the most part I find no interest in dialoging on theological issues. I have mailed a theological newsletter that I used to write to many of these pastors with the hope of creating an opportunity for dialogue. We also started CAPS (Compton Academy for Protestant Studies), with guests lecturers that include pastors and seminary professors, for the purpose of providing a non-threatening atmosphere where church history and the doctrines of the faith could be shared with clergy and laity. We make it a point to extend invitations to each Academy session to those in the immediate area and the greater Los Angeles area as well.

My point is that the theological shift undergone by Greater Union has distanced us from churches in our denomination, in our community, and within the black church community as a whole. This distance had been both insightful and painful. Insightful, because what has been revealed through these experiences is how relatively unimportant doctrine and theology are to what we call fellowship. I have had in-depth conversations in private settings with some of the pastors with whom we have broken fellowship.

Some of them have expressed concern for the doctrinal ignorance in the black church in particular and the evangelical church as a whole. Some have even acknowledged the "rightness" of some aspects of Reformed theology proper. But they have been reluctant to preach this doctrine or to implement it in the life of their respective churches. It has been painful discovering that tradition and culture have trumped doctrine as the basis for Christian fellowship. It was this discovery in the early years of the reforming process at Greater Union that made the cross-denominational fellowships between black Baptist, Pentecostal, and Word-Faith churches (commonplace in succeeding years) less surprising. In fact the early '90s saw the rise of the Full Gospel movement among black Baptists, replete with bishops.

When this Full Gospel movement was in its nascent phase, I put together a conference on the person and work of the Holy Spirit. I believed confusion on this central doctrine was what made the masses vulnerable to this spurious invasion. Prior to the conference I approached a number of influential pastors in an effort to get them and their members to attend—all to no avail. Indeed, ties have been severed within the circle of churches with which we previously had fellowship. Formerly solid personal friendships have dissolved because of the gospel and an effort to maintain a sense of doctrinal integrity. A solid understanding of Scripture makes it impossible to be surprised by this turn of events. And while I have learned some very important lessons, they nonetheless remain painful lessons indeed.

Summary

I've omitted many things in this telling of my personal journey into the doctrines of grace and the story of reforming work taking place at Greater Union. For instance, I have mentioned the fallout with other churches and pastors because of our shift. But there was significant fallout within the ranks as well. At one point we went from a church with steady numerical growth to a point where we lost at least three-quarters of our membership. And some of those that remained did so because (in their words),

"We were here when you came, and we'll be here when you're gone." Those were difficult and dark times. But God sustained me through his Word and the Holy Spirit. I was sustained through the prayers and support of a core group of believers within the church who saw these "new doctrines" and the gospel in all their beauty and comfort. I was sustained through the prayers, conversations, and words of encouragement of godly men and fellow pastors across the country. My brothers and co-hosts on *The White Horse Inn* were a great help. The faithful preaching, teaching, and friendships of men like R. C. Sproul, James Montgomery Boice, W. Robert Godfrey, James Williams, Earl Blackburn, and Greg Bero have been invaluable. The new members that have come to be a part of Greater Union, specifically because of the doctrines, have been a tremendous refreshment. The Lord has sent men, women, and families who are the firstfruits of a great gospel harvest. And of course my lovely wife, Lisa, who has seen and heard it all, has stood with me and knelt with and for me as we have labored for the gospel. She has been a model of grace enabling us to raise our son in those turbulent days without sowing seeds of resentment toward the church of Christ.

Greater Union is far from perfect or from being perfectly reformed. Some would say we are not Reformed enough. On the flipside, we will not appeal to others because we are not "black" enough in terms of our worship style and in the absence of programs and activities commonly associated with black churches. However, what I discovered on my personal journey was the gospel of grace as it is revealed in Scripture and centered in the person and work of Jesus Christ. My ongoing aim at Greater Union has been to infuse the gospel into every aspect of the church so that the glory of the triune God would be supreme in all things. As I listen to our children answer catechism questions, and as I listen to senior members rejoice over the doctrine of justification and its implications (even as they bemoan the fact that they had been in the church for many years without that knowledge), I have reason to believe the gospel has been heard and received. There is a myth that doctrine is not practical. But my ministry to people in some of life's most difficult and trying circumstances has proven otherwise. For those people, as with all of the saints through the years, Jesus is indeed real. Not because of anything they feel—although they feel at the deepest level—but because they have placed all of their trust in all of God's Word, where he reveals his Son. We are not ashamed of the gospel because it and it alone announces the power of God unto salvation. Has the journey been hard? Without a doubt, but "I wouldn't take nothing for my journey now!"

Soli Deo Gloria

6

I Remember It Well

MICHAEL LEACH

It was a time of love and gaiety; a time of romance and court-ship; a time of grace and genteelness, when men were men and women were women, when chivalry prevailed, and when gentle-men would open the car door for their ladies (after the car had stopped!). It was a time of musicals, of the ballad, when songs had words that were intelligent, intelligible, and repeatable. It was 1958, the year in which the Oscar-winning film *Gigi* premiered. "I Remember It Well" was one of its many popular melodies. Set against a backdrop of inoffensive one-upmanship, this innocu-ous, ironic ditty performed by multilingual French entertainer Maurice Chevalier and Hermione Gingold, amusingly describes their varying recollections of their first meeting.

Much has transpired since that time. Indeed the vast majority of intervening events has evanesced into clouds of forgetfulness. However, there are some experiences that linger with an ever-green freshness in our minds. Their impact persists with ongoing validity and force in our lives. Such events are defining. For me, at the top of this limited set of experiences lie my conversion and my introduction to Reformed theology.

A Reconciling Count and Theology

I remember the circumstances clearly. It wasn't 1958, it was 1991. Ah yes! I remember it well. We had just finished ministering to the inmates at the (then) Rankin County Correctional Facility in Pearl, Mississippi, when two important events occurred simultaneously: the inmate account was unreconciled, and the rainfall that had started earlier had intensified into a frightening thunderstorm. For those unfamiliar with the prison systems, correctional administrators live and die by the inmate count. They have to account for every inmate frequently, and when this tallying process is underway, doors are locked, gates are closed, and the facility is placed under "lock down." This means that all persons on the premises, whether inmate or visitor, must remain where they are while the calculations are being made. At the end of the tallying process, the numbers from each building are sent to the assistant warden in the main office for verification. Should the current count not correspond with the last, the entire process has to be repeated for as many times as it is necessary to secure a balancing of the inmate population. As if that one fact were not enough to detain us, the storm was raging with an uncommon ferocity such that, even if the count were reconciled, we would still be unable to leave. In this sense, we were doubly locked in: by the inaccurate count and by inclement weather.

While the guards were experiencing unusual difficulty in their numerical reconciliation, the members of our prison ministry and I engaged in conversation with the inmates. I was speaking with one of the inmates who worked in the chaplain's office when my attention was attracted to a wide collection of donated books and magazines lying on a huge desk at the rear of the chapel. I was casually scanning the front pages of a few not worthy of mentioning, when at the far end of the desk I saw a magazine that seemed to be compelling me to take it up and read. With indifferent inquisitiveness, I began to read a few lines of the first article. However, as I continued reading, more and more the author seemed to make sense; both his words and his meaning were gradually captivating. I stopped reading and turned to the cover of the magazine to find out its name, and there it was printed in a rather unobtrusive way: *Tabletalk*. *Tabletalk* is the monthly publication of Ligonier Ministries, which was founded and led by Dr. R. C. Sproul.

The more I read, the more I was consumed by the theology conveyed in that magazine. Up to that point I had never read any book or magazine containing such deep theological insights stated with such clarity and cogency. I quickly began to skim through the pages of other articles to verify their consistency, and I was not disappointed. I was now in high cotton—a Mississippi vernacular equivalent to hog heaven. By this time I was really consumed and was comfortably seated at the desk in order to more easily satiate my dogmatic enthusiasm. I was totally absorbed in my endeavor when my concentration was violated by the most disgustingly gauche words I had ever heard in my life: "Count clear!" These two words bellowed out by an irritated guard penetrated the air with an unpleasant firmness that reminded me of the purpose of my being there. The count was balanced, the storm had ceased, and it was time for us to leave.

That night I took the magazine home with me without official permission because the chaplain to whom it belonged, Wendy Hatcher, and I were close friends.[1] Regrettably, I can recall only that it was a 1990 publication; the month and date escape me.

Compared to current issues, the *Tabletalk* of nearly two decades ago was less flashy in its overall presentation: the pages were fewer and less glossy; the fonts were not as attractive; the pictures were not as captivating; the margins were wider; and the color schemes were not as impressive. Yet, this characteristic stands firm: the content has remained faithful to the doctrines of evangelicalism and true to the Reformed distinctives. *Tabletalk* continues to be a standard fare among students of Reformed theology.

R. C. Sproul's impact has been foundational in my life. I have purchased, read, listened to, and viewed a wide collection of his books and tapes. I continue to incorporate all media of his works into my pastoral office.

Sproul has a compendious knowledge of all matters, ranging from sports to philosophy to theology. He is equally authoritative in the minutiae of life as well as in broader, all-embracing subjects such as origin and destiny. Above all, he has earned the respect of his colleagues as well as his enemies. He is regarded as a man of integrity and as one of the most consistent, authoritative, and recognized voices on all branches of theology, especially that of the Reformed faith. I have cut my teeth on such of his written works as *Chosen by God*; *Knowing Scripture*; *Willing to Believe*; *The Holiness of God*; *Essential Truths of the Christian Faith*; the four-part series *Before the Face of God*; *Pleasing God*; and so on. In addition, I have been a keen student of some of his earlier audio series such as "Hath God Said?"; "God's Law and the Christian"; "Themes in Apologetics"; "The Battle for the Mind"; "The Doctrine of Christ, Parts 1 and 2"; "The Consequences of Ideas"; and many others. Today, the R. C. Sproul Digital Library is one of my most-referenced resources. I still subscribe to *Tabletalk*, attend Ligonier's conferences, listen to Sproul's international radio program, "Renewing Your Mind," and yes, purchase his material.

Through his teaching, my increased understanding of the Reformed faith impelled me to change my seminary from Liberty University School of Lifelong Learning in Lynchburg, Virginia, where I was an extended educational student, to the Reformed Theological Seminary of Jackson, Mississippi, from which I graduated in 1996. Also, my new allegiance necessitated a radical transformation of my library. Commentaries by Harry Ironside were promptly replaced by Matthew Henry's; writings by Oliver Greene were exchanged for those by James Montgomery Boice and by D. G. Barnhouse; Arno and Frank Gaebelein by Simon Kistemaker and William Hendriksen; Charles Stanley and Billy Graham by J. C. Ryle; Charles Ryrie by O. Palmer Robertson and Ed Clowney; and on and on. Later the works of Calvin, Luther, Warfield, Owen, Edwards, Charles and A. A. Hodge, and many other stalwarts of the Reformed tradition would occupy greater space in my home. My current group of authors and teachers has expanded to include one to whom I am very endeared, Sinclair

Ferguson, and along with him, John Piper and Michael Horton, and my former professors, J. Ligon Duncan III, Duncan Rankin, Dale Ralph Davis, and John Currid.

Simplification of Life

Since that fateful day in the prison my studies have been mainly focused on the historic doctrines of the Reformed faith and on the history of the Reformation. From this perspective, my life has been simplified. I have known many brothers and sisters who came to embrace the Reformed tradition after going through many dangers, toils, and snares in Word-Faith theology, liberation theology, Pentecostalism and neo-Pentecostalism, Afrocentric teachings, and many others. I thank the Lord that he has protected me from slipping into these injurious aberrations and for simplifying my theological life, in spite of my ongoing sin and self-inflicted struggles. He has faithfully enabled me to seek and to rejoice in both the sufficiency and simplicity that are to be found in Jesus Christ alone.

Major Impact

Well, what are some of the Reformed doctrines that have impacted me most? The answers are legion, but the doctrine of Christ bestrides them all like an imposing giant colossus. There is no other person in all of Scripture and in all of history who is as dominant and disparaged, perfect and spurned, good and despised, loving and rejected, as he is. No other religious faith teaches the self-revelation of God in the weakness of human flesh. No other holds to the doctrine of God, who lowered himself to live among his creatures, undergoing all of their experiences, except for sin, and then paying the penalty for their sin with his life. No other religion or faith can claim such a profound history of redemption. None other dares to contemplate at the same time the vast disparity and immeasurable distance between Creator and creature, between a holy God and sinful man, as well as the nearness of God and man, the very bridging of this gap by our Mediator, the God-Man, Jesus Christ himself. This doctrine of

Christ, a *sine qua non* of biblical Christianity, reaches its fullest exposition in the traditions of the Reformed faith. Even at this time of writing, I would rather deviate from my outline and apply myself to this topic, the majesty and glory of Jesus Christ. Unwillingly, I take leave of this strong inclination.

Next, I strongly believe that the doctrine of God is also crucial to our time. An accurate understanding of God as he declares himself in Holy Scripture, as the God who reveals himself to us by his divine attributes and properties, which attain the apex of his self-disclosure in Christ, is all but lost and despised in our culture. Postmodernism, with its relentless promotion of anti-foundationalism, is increasing its sinuous and sinister penetration into the church and is particularly being manifest in the teachings of Open Theism, Prosperity Gospel, and to some degree the emergent church. While it is true that each of these deviations has its own peculiarities, they all have this one common pervasive thread: foundationally they are all attacks on the character of God. Not only do they distort the divine attributes depicted in Scripture, but they also too often discard the historical church's understanding of them, most of which are captured in the creeds and confessions faithfully handed down to us by our forefathers.

About two decades ago the prevalent aspect of this ungodly assault on God and on Scripture was framed by the question, "Has God said?" Like the serpent's words to Eve in the garden of Eden, seducing her to believe his demonic lies rather than the truth of the Word of God, the aberrant teaching of yesteryear constituted a frontal attack on the very authority of God. Today, this attack continues with the addition of a few subtle twists. In this scenario, *God is still speaking, but he is speaking different words*, so to speak. To the Open Theists, God speaks not on the basis of ultimate, absolute, and perfect knowledge but on the basis of a knowledge that is limited, one that is contingent upon and conditioned by man's actions in history. To the Prosperity and Word-Faith proponents, God's Word is not his condemnation of man for sin and his provision of his eternal Son as his only acceptable, propitiatory sacrifice for sin, but a promise of the good life, health, and wealth, with some tidbits of spirituality tossed in for good measure. As one of the more visible proponents of this false teaching has written, we can and we must live our best life now.[2] Where the emergent church advocates are concerned, a new "conversation" is being undertaken in a very fluid and continuously emerging environment sometimes called a village. In this milieu, what is of utmost importance is not the objective propositions enshrined in Scripture and received and cherished by the historical church but a decentralized interfaith dialog aimed at achieving a widespread ecumenism, driven by an incentive to build the kingdom by reaching the world through the process of storytelling.

The point is that all of these distortions blatantly reject the centrality of the gospel message as it is reflected in the person and work of Jesus Christ. Modern "reasoning" holds that, in order to meet the demands of contemporary culture, God must speak a new word in new ways. The essence of these renegade doctrines is a concentrated assault on God, whose word is forever settled in heaven (Ps. 119:89) and who continues to speak to his chosen covenant people by his Word and Spirit. From Genesis to Revelation, his message is the same. He offers salvation by grace alone through faith alone in the sinless life of the God-man, Jesus Christ alone.

Yet, as crucial as this doctrine of God is for all evangelicalism, and as staunchly as the Reformed faith has stood in its defense, I continue to find overwhelming and humbling encouragement within the doctrine of divine election.[3] This has had enormous impact on my life.

Divine Election

A tautology is an unnecessary and meaningless statement in which the same idea is repeated. For example, the statement "all husbands have wives" is tautological because by definition only husbands have wives and also because by definition one could not be a husband if one did not have a wife.[4] In this construction the second part of the sentence neither clarifies nor intensifies the meaning contained in the first; it is a needless addition. I remember my friend's son once peppering him with questions typical of the pattern of three- or four-year-olds. As soon as my friend would answer one question, his son would raise the very bothersome monosyllabic question, "Why?" After about eight rounds of intense questions and answers, my friend, not known for his patience and characteristically showing signs of exasperation, blurted out a terminal tautological response to his puzzled child: "It is green because it is green! And that's it." (Here we have the situation of the bull muzzling the calf when he was treading his corns!) The fatherly intent was clearly understood and reluctantly acted upon: you have reached the end of all filial inquiries.

How markedly different is it with God, the ultimate Father, in his dealing with sinners! In the realm of redemption, in order for sinful man to enjoy the fullness of blessing that God wants to share with him, fallen man's inability to seek God must be overcome at all points by a gracious, merciful, and omnipotent divine initiative. This pattern is shown throughout Scripture, but the specific passage I have in mind is Deuteronomy 7:6–8, a key Old Testament passage demonstrating the sovereign role of God in choosing or electing his covenant people unto himself:

> For you are a people holy to the LORD your God. The LORD your God has chosen you to be a people for his treasured possession, out of all the peoples who are on the face of the earth. It was not because you were more in number than any other people that the LORD set his love on you and chose you, for you were the fewest of all peoples, but it is because the LORD loves you and is keeping the oath that he swore to your fathers, that the LORD has brought you out with a mighty hand and redeemed you from the house of slavery, from the hand of Pharaoh king of Egypt.[5]

While the doctrine of election is common to biblical Christianity, the fullness as well as the consistency of its implications are most honored and embraced by the Reformed faith. Man's radical inability and God's free and sovereign decision to save some by his grace alone comprise a dualism that can only be overcome or breached by God's monergistic act of regeneration. This essential truth is abundantly stressed by Benjamin B. Warfield, who writes:

> Thus it comes about that the doctrine of monergistic regeneration—or as it was phrased by the older theologians, of "irresistible grace" or "effectual calling"—is the hinge of the Calvinistic soteriology, and lies much more deeply embedded in the system than the doctrine of predestination itself which is popularly looked upon as its hall-mark. . . . There is accordingly nothing against which Calvinism sets its face with more firmness than every form and degree of autosoterism. Above everything else, it is determined that God, in His Son Jesus Christ, acting through the Holy Spirit whom He has sent, shall be recognized as our veritable Saviour. . . . This is the root of Calvinistic soteriology; and it is because this deep sense of human helplessness and this profound consciousness of indebtedness for all that enters [sic] into salvation to the free grace of God is the root of its soteriology that to it the doctrine of election becomes the *cor cordis* of the Gospel.[6]

The Particularity of Divine Election

In looking more closely at Deuteronomy 7:6–8, a few observations are in order. First, verse 6 sets up the proposition by reminding Israel of her covenant separation (holy) unto the Lord. It recalls the very words and meaning of Exodus 19:5–6, in which the Lord confers the threefold status of treasured possession, priesthood, and holy nation upon her in the context of a covenant relationship after he had single-handedly redeemed her from Egypt. While it is true that the entire earth and everything in it belong to God (Ps. 24:1), his sovereign choice of Israel as his own people highlights the particularity of the divine act and of the relationship. Israel belongs to God in a way that is different from the other nations. It is an ownership that is not only determined by creation but also that is defined by redemption (1 Cor. 6:19–20). God's sovereign election of Israel as his treasured possession means that Israel belongs to him completely, exclusively, and uniquely.[7] *It is a relationship in which God will brook no rival. It is a description that bespeaks the zeal or jealousy of the Lord for his people. Israel's stipulated covenant role in this relationship is one of unwavering obedience and total dependence upon Yahweh, her Creator and Redeemer, her Lord and Master.*

The Radical Unworthiness of Man

Second, verses 7 and 8 underscore the absolute unworthiness of Israel as God's choice. "It was not because you were more in number than any other people that the Lord set his love on you and chose you, for you were the fewest of all peoples" (Deut. 7:7) comes very close to being a condemnation. Lest Israel be tempted to pride herself on the size of her population, the expansion of her progeny, and the might of her people, these solemn words were intended to have a kenotic effect upon her. They stripped her of all ground of boasting before God. She had no inherent quality and no intrinsic worth that would incline the Lord to choose her. As if these destroyers of Israel's hubris were not enough, the Lord next asserted her nothingness by declaring the wonderful tautology: "the LORD set his love on you and chose you . . . because the LORD loves you" (Deut. 7:8).[8]

Here is the great affirmation that all of salvation is all of God. Here is the great Reformed insistence on the clear biblical teaching of the radical depravity of man, on his condition of original sin in which he is dead, that is, completely spiritually unresponsive to all the things of God. Nothing inheres in the creature to incline, motivate, or cause the sovereign God to even want him. Indeed, apart from Christ, our best works are as abominable as soiled menstrual cloths (Isa. 64:6).

What an astounding statement! What a crippling statement! What an encouraging statement! How can this be encouraging? It is heartening because it reminds us that like Israel, we are entirely passive in God's salvation of our souls. We contribute nothing to our regeneration by the Holy Spirit. It is God himself who foreknew, predestined, and chose us in Christ to be his covenant people before the foundation of the earth. This he did by contemplating us, his elect, of all the nations of the earth, out of the *massa peccati,* the mass of sin, and then by his sovereign decree alone, electing us in Christ to be his own personal possession.

The Covenant Faithfulness of God

Third, the rest of verse 8 reinforces the truth of Israel's natural unworthiness from a slightly different perspective. God's redemption of Israel has a remote dimension. He had delivered her from Egypt and Pharaoh in order to fulfill a covenant pledge he had made to her forefather long before she was even born. This sounds like a Deuteronomic anticipation of Romans 9:11, in which the apostle Paul explains that God's sovereign, free choice of Jacob unto salvation and his rejection of Esau, despite the fact that both brothers were of unquestionable Jewish pedigree, was made for the only reason that his divine purpose in election might be established. Israel was therefore twice reminded of her unworthiness, namely of her redemption as the product of divine sovereign election and of the fulfillment of God's patriarchal promise. She therefore had no claim against God.

This is the unchanging historical pattern with which God deals with sinners. This is the wondrous biblical truth of divine election that the Reformers so adamantly developed and defended. Yet, there is a greater dimension to be grasped, namely that all God's actions in creation and especially in redemption are designed to bring him the glory he so richly deserves and so steadfastly demands.

To the Glory of God Alone

After cataloging God's marvelous work in bringing Gentile and Jew together in one church, Paul punctuates his doxological outburst with "from him and through him and to him are all things. To him be glory forever. Amen" (Rom. 11:36). This is the conclusion of the whole matter: in the exercise of the vast riches of his deep wisdom and knowledge, his unfathomable judgments and inscrutable ways, God has designed that his sovereign work in election would glorify him above all.

The Reformed faith correctly regards this principle as the grand rubric under which all else is subsumed. To this end, the Reformation slogan *soli Deo gloria* is considered the all-embracing principle controlling all others. It strives to promote God's glory in all matters as the central thrust of life. The first question of the Westminster Shorter Catechism affirms that man's primary purpose in life is to enjoy God and to glorify him forever. According to Warfield, Calvinism or Reformed theology not only asks how shall a man be saved but above all ponders, "How shall God be glorified?" In Warfield's assessment, this is a system of doctrine that "begins, . . . centers, [and] ends with the vision of God in his glory: and it sets itself before all things to render to God His rights in every sphere of life-activity."[9]

Ministerial Experience

The ministerial road travelled since that eventful evening in Mississippi has been rocky but rewarding, extremely challenging but immensely consoling; after all, we are not living in times characterized by a massive outpouring of fervent desire to hear and grasp life-changing truth.

In 1996 I assumed my first pastorate at Canton Bible Baptist Church in Canton, Mississippi. My cautious steps toward the gradual implementation of Reformed teaching were met with varied responses. I resolved that the best method was to proclaim Reformed doctrines formally in preaching and teaching and informally, when afforded the opportunity, in private conversations, counseling sessions, and family visitations, naturally flowing from the explicit and implicit context of biblical expression. For the most part, such teaching was received with joy and gratitude. Nevertheless, there was a minority group whose representative accused me of "bringing Presbyterian doctrine into the church." Overall, during the three years I served at Canton Bible Baptist Church, the Lord provided an ample measure of success, evidenced in part by an increasing desire of his people to hear the Word of God accurately proclaimed and by the liberty that this gospel message engendered among them.

Following graduation from Reformed Theological Seminary, I moved to the Atlanta area to begin the work of church planting. My experience as a church planter here, however, has been quite different. Most of the African-American churches in this sweltering reserve of fluid eclecticism have their own brand of theology. It is a waning residual of historic orthodoxy; an unquestioned default system of Arminianism, with heavy influences by the Prosperity Gospel and Word-Faith teachings; deep inroads by local and national politics, especially that of the National Democratic Party; and deep encrustations of the Civil Rights Movement. It maintains many troubling aspects of liberation theology evidenced by the growing popular appeal of Afrocentrism and the Feminist Gospel. There is also a continuing retreat from the transcendent supernaturalism of biblical theology into an entrenched liberalism known for its commitment to pragmatism, the Social Gospel, and the confusing of the church with (and even its submergence under) the broader stratum of the community. Against this volatile backdrop, planting a Reformed church has close affinity with a suicidal attempt; it strongly resembles an adventurous quixotic undertaking.

Here the faithful have been small in number. In many cases their embrace of Reformation teaching has caused rifts with family and church members and has brought them the unjust accusations of cult associations and yes, of buying into "a white man's doctrine." Yet, we press on. We are beginning to witness a small turning away from popular theology, and indications are that this trickle is slowly increasing. The Lord is drawing his people out from their "churches" and pointing many of them to churches such as ours. We stand firmly convinced in our calling and, by his grace alone, will keep on striving to make this calling sure.

I am grateful that Reformation theology, with its typically unyielding faithfulness to Scripture, is most faithful in developing the implications of the two fundamental extremities: man's radical corruption and God's free, sovereign election. I am thankful that the Reformed faith emphasizes most consistently that *all* of salvation is of God alone. I am humbled beyond measure by the divine foreordination that I would be shut in with inmates on a dark and stormy Mississippi night in order that the Lord would shine his light in my heart ever so brightly through the articles of that old *Tabletalk* magazine. I am not deserving of God's gracious overtures toward me and for fore-arranging and using all of these events as his providential instruments to usher in a climacteric in my life. I am humbled that God would allow me to personally experience the reality of *post tenebras, lux* (the Reformation slogan meaning "after darkness comes light") by his grace alone and all to his glory alone. I am exceedingly thankful for the mystery and mercy of divine election.

All of his mercies, I remember well.

7

The Old Bait and Switch

LANCE LEWIS

We've all been lied to, manipulated, flimflammed, and conned. We've been bamboozled. And in my mind, it became increasingly clear that the one guilty of such deception in my life was the living God. I was preached to, told, and taught that Jesus Christ offered me salvation if I'd only put my faith in him. I was told that whosoever believed in Christ would not perish but have everlasting life. I was told to come to the Lord for salvation, but it seemed that all I did was fall for the ultimate bait and switch. The more and more I learned about my supposed great salvation, the more and more it felt like lifelong probation.

I soon discovered that what I'd been taught was that the Lord didn't really give me salvation as much as I was granted the opportunity to get it for myself. At first it seemed easy. All I had to do was act right—all the time, for my entire life. Still, even that didn't appear that tall of an order. The older saints at church seemed to have it down pat. Come to church, read your Bible, shout real loud, and come to church some more. I picked up the local dialect and was soon fluent in mid-twentieth century Christianese with a

Pentecostal accent. This was going to be a breeze. However, there was the sin that did Lance in. What sin, you ask? Name one: anger, bitterness, resentment, lust, pride, gossip, sowing discord, dishonoring God's name, lying, covetousness, and a host of others. A few years after coming into "the church" I was, as a friend of mine would say, in deep, deep yogurt. On the one hand, I knew what I was supposed to do in order to gain eternal life. On the other hand, there was one small problem. I couldn't do it. True, I could fool others into thinking I was doing it, and on occasion I even fooled myself. I never considered myself a hypocrite nor was I playing a game. I wanted to do right. I wanted to live holy. I wanted to know for sure that God loved me, accepted me, and favored me; but looking at my life I knew that he was displeased, and I dreaded the day I would finally have to face him.

After years of trying to genuinely and enthusiastically walk with the Lord, I felt like I had been lied to, manipulated, flim-flammed, conned, and bamboozled. My peers were of little help. They too struggled in the faith, with many dropping like early autumn leaves as soon as the pressures of life and the temptations of sin grew too much. It seemed as though we lived for the next revival, the next conference, the next play, the next concert, the next retreat, anything that would infuse us with a shot of spiritual power that would propel us from this life into the next. So there I was, resigned to a life that was little more than a big question mark. Would God accept me into his eternal kingdom? Maybe he would, maybe not. The best I could do was the best I could do, and hope for the best.

A Series of Unconventional Providences

But then the Lord had mercy on me. I had sensed the call to ministry, and like other young ministers I knew, I began busily reading and studying Scripture. And then it began to happen. Reading through Scripture I began to wonder about one of my church's core beliefs. Having come to faith in a Pentecostal church, I was taught and had accepted the Pentecostal conviction of the baptism of the Spirit. I too taught it to others and encouraged them to seek the baptism of the Spirit. There was always, however, one slight catch. I never seemed to have the experience that Spirit-baptism was supposed to deliver; neither did some of my closest friends, or the vast majority of the young adult group I hung with. We were all faking the funk and all answering the weekly sacramental Sunday altar call.

As I studied Scripture regarding the baptism of the Spirit as taught by my church, I came to the conclusion that what I had believed just wasn't so. The book, *Baptism and Fullness*, by John Stott proved to be one of the most helpful books during my study. This was the first book I read by someone who was a Bible-believing Christian and who laid out a biblical case against something I took for granted as absolute truth. It would not be the last.

In God's providence, I actually got to study Spirit-baptism in one of our adult Sunday school classes. We had been studying church history, including the history of our denomination. We then began a study on some of the core doctrines of our church. Time and again I found myself questioning some of the things that everyone else seemingly accepted without question. Though I wasn't deemed a heretic, it was clear by the end of our study that I no longer accepted or believed in the baptism of the Spirit as taught by the vast majority of Pentecostals. Suddenly, things got really interesting.

Our teacher decided that after studying some of our beliefs, we would delve into a few things we did not believe. That was fine with me, since for the past few weeks I had taken another look at these things called election and predestination. I had heard of these teachings before and had outright and with great fervor rejected them as doctrines of demons. How in the world could God be fair if he arbitrarily chose some for salvation and passed over others? Yet, I couldn't seem to read the first several verses of Ephesians 1 without the sinking feeling that God had done just that. Thankfully, I was in a class that would straighten these things out. We began studying the doctrines of predestination and eternal security with the expectation that God was fair in his dealings with men and that our salvation was as secure as we decided to make it.

The Light Breaks In

However, the more we studied, the more troubled I became. At first I didn't tell anyone of this, not even my wife. This could not be happening. God could not have the right to predetermine my destiny based solely on his own good will and pleasure, could he? In regard to "once saved, always saved," we know that someone made that up just to have an excuse to dive headlong into a life of sin and debauchery, right? Finally I began to open up to my wife that we may have had this election thing wrong. While it didn't make natural sense, it appeared that God chose us for salvation before the world began and without any input or inclination on our part. One by one my objections faded away as the true grace of God broke into my heart and mind.

After telling my wife, we decided to share this with my best friend Kevin Smith. Kevin and I had been running buddies before we got saved. By God's grace we came to faith together, went to the same church together, left that church and joined another Pentecostal church together, and even spent one semester at a branch campus of Penn State together. I remember the two of us taking the long bus ride from Broad and Olney up to Abington and listening to R. W. Shambach on the radio (yes, this was the Stone Age before mp3, Discmans, or Walkmans). Kev and I had drawn swords together and battled with those in our college fellowship who insisted on eternal security. For every passage our friends brought up supporting it, we'd remind them that though the blood wouldn't burn, they most surely would if they turned their backs on the Lord. Nevertheless, I later became convinced of the truth of unconditional election.

I knew when I told Kevin that our close fellowship would come to an end. I forget how we struck up the conversation, but eventually I told Kev my conclusion and that I was going to share it with the class soon. Once more the God of heaven and earth surprised me. While I had been struggling through and embracing unconditional election, Kevin had become convinced of the reality of the preservation of the saints. Along with our wives we began to talk, compare notes, and read, and pretty soon it became clear that there was no going back. Once we grabbed hold of unconditional election and the preservation of the saints, the doctrines of total depravity, limited atonement, and irresistible grace soon followed.

So there we were again. The pride of West Philly had once again drawn swords, but this time in the defense of biblical Reformed theology. It soon became clear that we would have to leave our present church. For one thing Kevin was being asked to lead the youth and young adult ministry, and I was already teaching and coordinating the teenage Bible study. Moreover, we had both answered the call to ministry and believed that God had called us into pastoral ministry. We spoke with our pastor, who graciously accepted our reason for leaving, and we soon left that fellowship on very good terms. I remain convinced that the believers there were genuine people of God who wanted to know and serve the Lord. Kevin now serves as the senior pastor of Pinelands Presbyterian Church in Miami.

Through the Looking Glass

Leaving, however, brought up another issue. Where do we go to church? We didn't know anyone who was Reformed, and there wasn't an abundance of Reformed churches in our neighborhood. Kevin suggested that we check out this church in downtown Philly where he had attended a theology conference. Walking into historic Tenth Presbyterian Church was like walking through the looking glass. It seemed that everything they did was strange and different from the way we had experienced Christianity for the past nine years. One of my first thoughts was, *We'll never fit in here.* Thus I soon asked if this denomination had any black churches. "Oh yes, we do," was the response. "We have two of them."

"So, you have just two black Reformed churches in the city?" I asked.

"Uh, no," was the reply. "There are two black churches in the entire denomination."

One was somewhere in central Jersey and the other in Baltimore. We resigned ourselves to sitting down, hanging back, and enjoying the rich teaching we were treated to each Sunday. At that time, the pastor was Dr. James Montgomery Boice. Dr. Boice was working his way through the letter to the Romans. Each message seemed to reinforce the goodness, plan, wisdom, power, and grace of God. Did we miss many of the aspects of our old church? Yes, we did. But there's something about the Word of the living God. We were blessed to be at Tenth while Dr. Boice preached through the latter half of Romans 8. It was just what I needed. Hearing the Word of God, I discovered that he hadn't lied to, manipulated, flim-flammed, conned, or bamboozled me.

So Great a Salvation

God had chosen me to be with him in salvation before the foundation of the world. His choice was motivated by his unconditional, redemptive love for me. Having chosen me, he called me to himself through the preaching of the gospel. Upon my answering the call of the gospel, God justified me. He gave me the perfect right standing that Christ earned and at the same time forgave all of my sin because Christ took my punishment on the cross. But God wasn't finished. Those whom he loved before the world began, he also predestined to become the sons of his delight. Those whom he predestined, he called; those he called, he justified; and those he justified, he glorified (Rom. 8:30). Say what? My standing and salvation were so secure, it was if I were already standing before the throne worshiping the Lamb! No wonder they called it amazing grace. For the first time in my walk with the Lord I could enjoy him without the nagging feeling that somehow he was displeased with me and that one way or another he was going to let me have it.

I grew accustomed to Tenth's worship, sopping up God's Word, and in general I was content to take in the teaching and fellowship with the saints. But the Lord who loved and called me wasn't having any of that. He didn't open my eyes and heart to the precious truths of his salvation for me to sit on them like a greedy miser counting his treasure. At Tenth God began to prepare me for the work of the ministry I was to pursue in the years to come.

It soon became obvious that Reformed churches had about as many black folks in them as did the Philadelphia trade unions. Why was this, I wondered? I knew hundreds, perhaps thousands, of black folks who rode the weekly roller coaster of feel-good faith. Most were quite sincere, but for them Christianity seemed a crapshoot. They daily rolled the dice with their lives hoping that the "rapture" happened while they were in church worshiping the Lord.

The Souls of Black Folk

I believed that many of these dear souls would listen and adhere to the sound teaching of the doctrines of grace if they were ever exposed to them. However, it was likely that only a small fraction would make the leap from the black church into the context in which I had placed myself. It soon became clear that if African-Americans were to hear of, embrace, and live by the teachings of grace, someone would have to bring it to them in their neighborhoods and in a way that was familiar to them. Even before embracing Reformed theology, I had sensed a definite call to start a church that would feature strong biblical teaching, consistent, sustained, and compassionate outreach, and a genuine warm, accepting fellowship. What started out as a call, however, soon grew to be a lifelong imperative. And yet there was still much to learn—not only about Reformed theology, but about myself, my people, and the Lord who chose, called, saved, and would one day send me.

Having few black role models to draw from, I leaned heavily on those good white brothers who spoke and wrote about Reformed theology. Along with Dr. Boice, there was D. Martyn Lloyd-Jones, R. C. Sproul, J. I. Packer, and others. Reading them and listening to others led me into other aspects of Reformed theology. Like many, I learned that the doctrines of grace are only the beginning. Reformed theology presents a coherent, organized understanding of salvation and life from a true biblical perspective. For example, I learned that the Old Testament wasn't just a disjointed collection of stories that served mainly as examples of what and what not to do. I was taught that God's plan of salvation was in effect long before Jesus was born of the virgin Mary. I also discovered that what I had come to know as salvation wasn't just confined to eternal fire insurance. Looking back I remember questioning this at both of the Pentecostal churches I belonged to. It also seemed that we should have had more of a connection with the community our church was a part of.

A good brother named Carl Ellis helped me to see these things more clearly when I first heard him speak in 1993. He spoke on issues of justice, racial reconciliation, and the kingdom of God in ways I had not heard before. Carl helped me to make the connections between my theology and how it related to those I was called to serve. With brother Carl's help, I came to see how I could make a definite impact on my people and why it was important to do so. Listening to Carl whet my appetite for seeing a unified church with people from various ethnicities pursuing their Lord and engaging their community. Carl affirmed that the goal of our salvation was the glory of God, and that this glory was seen in God's character, nature, and ways as expressed fully in the person and work of Jesus Christ.

The "T" Word

One of the events that contributed to how I thought about ministry within God's church was Dr. Boice's call to a broad group of evangelicals to challenge the wider church to return to its mission of proclaiming God's law as the only standard of righteousness and the gospel of Jesus Christ as the only message of salvation. I recall a meeting Dr. Boice had with the leaders of Tenth during a weekend retreat in the early nineties (I had been ordained a deacon by then) where he expressed grave concern over the worldly direction in which the church was heading.

Dr. Boice's concern and call to action coincided with a book written by David Wells entitled *No Place for Truth or Whatever Happened to Evangelical Theology*. Reading that book, listening to Dr. Boice, and checking out the brothers on the radio program *The White Horse Inn* helped me to think through the impact of culture on the mission, ministry, and truth of God's church. I was also challenged to consider the importance of theology in the life of every church and believer.

These were the thoughts and issues that weighed on my mind as I sought to work through how what I believed would affect my life and ministry. To that end, I began to have a greater appreciation for the worship at Tenth. I came to Tenth believing that worship was basically my time to give God praise so that I could enjoy a blessing from him. I gave little thought for what happened in worship, what elements should be part of worship, and why we worshiped the way we did. I took it for granted that what we sang, how we responded, and even the delivery of the message was for the purpose of stirring my emotions. Looking more deeply into the Scriptures and discovering God's redemptive purpose for his people opened my eyes to see the need for and beauty of a service of worship that intentionally emphasized the character, nature, and ways of God as expressed fully in the person and work of Jesus Christ. It began to dawn on me that worship wasn't just a free-for-all; the goal wasn't to send praises up so that blessings could come down. I more and more discovered the connection between the way one worshiped and the way one thought about, delighted in, and served the living God. I began to grow concerned that the way I was introduced to and taught the faith, though well-meaning, was too man-centered. It lent itself too much to having God revolve around me, my agenda, and my blessings. And this wasn't something confined to the black church experience. *No Place for Truth* and Wells's following book, *God in the Wasteland: The Reality of Truth in a World of Fading Dreams,* informed me that this was an American church phenomenon.

I also began to grasp how biblical theology should affect the way one thinks, speaks, and lives. I came to learn that what one believes about Scripture, God, mankind, sin, salvation, Jesus Christ, the Holy Spirit, and the many other foundational truths the Bible teaches will inevitably affect the way he views and relates to the Lord. Despite what current evangelical thought would have us believe, theology is important. This reality came home one day as Kevin and I were talking about friends from our old churches. A good deal of them had for one reason or another fallen away from the faith. We spoke of how the regular trials of life and the lack of any comprehensive teaching and preaching made them easy pickings for the evil one. Moreover, we talked about the general lack of growth and change among God's people, Reformed and not Reformed. All theology is practical theology, if by "practical" you mean that what you learn and know about God shapes and directs the way you worship him, walk before him, and witness to the gospel of his Son, Jesus Christ. Theology isn't just a bunch of empty platitudes, nor is it just the purview of stuff-shirted white men in seminary. What we learn, know, accept, and believe about God will directly affect the way we view him, work, conduct ourselves in marriage, relate to others, deal with conflict, and handle suffering and sorrow.

Integration, Separation, or Assimilation

These were some of the initial ways Reformed theology shaped how I thought about life and ministry when we moved from Philadelphia to Virginia. We moved in order to pursue full-time ministry in a church plant, while attending seminary. Doing so also caused me to grapple with another issue that had been with me since accepting Reformed theology as my own, namely the issue of race and ethnicity. This issue was never far from my mind as I grew to learn more and more about Reformed theology. In talking to people regarding the lack of African-American Reformed churches and people within the ranks of the Reformed camp, I discovered that there were many reasons for this. Unfortunately there didn't appear to be many solutions to this dilemma. Race and ethnicity had been a subject of discussion among black and white evangelical Christians for some time. This in-family discussion was fueled by men like John Perkins, who in the early seventies had made racial reconciliation a core aspect of his ministry. Along with this the Promise Keepers movement of the early nineties placed a priority on racial reconciliation in its ministry toward men. The mid-nineties also witnessed the official repentance of the Southern Baptist Convention for the part their denomination played in promoting segregation up through the 1960s. Among Reformed churches, I knew of one in Chattanooga, Tennessee, called New City Fellowship, planted and pastored by Randy Nabors. It had taken the lead in promoting racial reconciliation within the PCA.

Racial reconciliation became one of the theological issues that dominated my outlook toward ministry for the next few years. I became more and more convinced that if the church of the Lord Jesus Christ in general and the Reformed church in particular was to demonstrate the reality of the gospel then we must pursue racial reconciliation as a top priority. Once more Carl Ellis gave some valuable input concerning some of the biblical ways the church could chart a course for authentic racial reconciliation. Consequently, and largely due to Ellis's influence (he had actually served as an assistant pastor of New City Fellowship with Randy Nabors), I took a position as a long-term pastoral intern with a church plant that was modeled after New City. In fact, it was my time at that church that led me to see that while racial reconciliation is an important factor in the lives of black folks, it wasn't the most pressing challenge we faced.

Nathan McCall's book, *What's Going On*, contains essays on the subject of race in America. He titled one of the chapters "Faking the Funk: The Middle-Class Black Folks of Prince Georges County." The theme of this chapter was the way in which the children of educated, middle-class African-Americans who had good jobs and lived in large, modern suburban homes chose to consciously model the attitude and behavior of economically poorer black young people who live in the poor areas of America's large cities. I experienced this phenomena when I moved my family from West Philadelphia to a townhome in the suburbs of central Virginia. I discovered that young black people who lived in nice homes and went to good suburban schools purposely chose to embrace the mindset of anti-intellectualism, anti-integration, anti-achievement, and anti-authority that affects many poor African-American young people who live in the poor neighborhoods of our large cities.

By saying this I do not mean that ethnicity did not play any part in the challenges faced by young African-Americans. However, in observing suburban black folks in Virginia it became clear to me that the social challenges facing African-Americans had less and less to do with racism and more with how we viewed ourselves and God—and what approach we were going to use in facing our challenges in this country.

A New Threat

As a pastor, and especially one who embraced the Reformed tradition, it became my practice to view the challenges faced by latter twentieth-century black folks in terms of the theology we embraced and believed. Though there were many complex social challenges, it appeared to me that the root of these challenges were theological rather than sociological in nature. It was the black church that was a refuge for the souls of black people during our subjugation in slavery and the virulent, brutal, and wicked racism that followed. The church that was our refuge through the decades of racial terrorism blossomed into the church of militant peaceful engagement under the direction of Martin Luther King Jr. and others. It was this church that carried our hopes for a future in which black people wouldn't just be treated like Americans, but treated as people created in God's image. By God's grace and power and through his sovereign providence, he worked through many believers who claimed allegiance to Jesus Christ and recognized that the press for biblical social justice was a godly thing to do.

However, once the initial gains of the Civil Rights Movement were obtained, the church lost its footing. Moving from the turbulent sixties into the mellow seventies, the black church was adrift in a cultural sea in which though the dragon of legal segregation was defeated, black folks still struggled with a litany of social, political, economic, emotional, and *theological* issues. As Bill Cosby said at an event marking the fiftieth year of the historic *Brown v. Board of Education* decision, "What . . . good is *Brown* if nobody wants an education!" The black church that was so strong in the face of virulent racism in the sixties struggled to come up with adequate answers to the growing pathologies gripping black people in the seventies and eighties.

The dawn of the nineties brought a new theology to the black church, though it was one that had lurked on the fringes for decades. This theology wasn't centered in the black church's historic poles of social justice or personal holiness but in health, wealth, prosperity, comfort, and conquest. This theology was radically individualistic, wildly popular, masterfully deceptive, and devastatingly effective. It was a theology that ripped the focus off of the historic person and work of Jesus Christ and placed the wants, wishes, and whims of people as the central cause of God, Scripture, salvation, and the Holy Spirit.

Ironically, the popular prosperity and health and wealth theology has revealed a few positive things. First, it demonstrates that black people were willing to adopt new ways of thinking regarding black church culture. Second, it shows that most black churchgoers welcomed integration and would gladly listen and follow white church leaders. Third, and perhaps most importantly, it shows that a new theology could be introduced into the black community. This is significant because it proves that what people believe about God, Scripture, mankind, sin, salvation, the person and work of Jesus Christ, the ministry of the Spirit, and the church matters. In other words, theology matters. Everyone has a theology. The issue is whether that theology is biblical. Does it arise from what Scripture says about the nature, character, ways, and will of God Almighty? Does it highlight, emphasize, and promote the person and work of Jesus Christ as the point, theme, substance, subject, main plot, main character, and culmination of life, Scripture, history, and salvation? Does it rightly see and define salvation as deliverance and rescue from God's anger against sin and those who practice it or view it as a ticket to our best life now? Is the end goal of that theology God's glory or man's pride, prosperity, and self-glory?

A Better Way

While no theology or theological system is perfect, it has been my conviction for the last eighteen years that biblically Reformed theology best sums up what Scripture says regarding the essence of God's person, worship, ways, will, rule, agenda, and salvation as expressed fully in the person and work of Jesus Christ. Reformed theology begins where any creature should begin in our exploration and study of God: with God himself. Also, biblical Reformed theology ends where any and every creature's study of God should end: with a humble acknowledgment and focus on the overall glory of God. In between these two poles Reformed theology attempts to teach and show the biblical connections between our creation, fall, judgment, and redemption by our Savior Jesus Christ. Biblically Reformed theology teaches that the salvation and reconciliation of humanity into a right relationship with God is the story of Scripture. And throughout that story biblically Reformed theology highlights the sovereignty, providence, beauty, order, justice, righteousness, faithfulness, goodness, wrath, compassion, mercy, grace, love, and salvation of that God.

Why must we hold to and promote this theology? We must do so because it is the truth. It is the truth about God, his Son, and his salvation. We must do so because it brings glory to God. I am in full agreement with the answer to the first question of the Westminster Shorter Catechism. That question is: "What is the chief end of man?" The answer: "Man's chief end is to glorify God and enjoy him forever." We must do so because black people will find ourselves, our dignity, our purpose, and our destiny only when we confess and agree with the song of the apostle Paul in Romans 11:

Oh, the depth of the riches and wisdom and knowledge of God! How unsearchable are his judgments and how inscrutable his ways!

"For who has known the mind of the Lord,
  or who has been his counselor?"
"Or who has given a gift to him
  that he might be repaid?"

For from him and through him and to him are all things. To him be glory forever. Amen. (Rom. 11:33–36)

8

The Doors of the Church Are Opened!

LOUIS C. LOVE JR.

Anyone who has spent any time in an African-American Missionary Baptist church has experienced the time in the order of service called "the invitation" or "the call to discipleship." This follows hard after the morning sermon. The pastor stands behind the pulpit and announces that "the doors of the church are opened!" The opportunity has arrived for people to "join church." Two or three deacons pick up a couple of pre-designated chairs and place them just in front of the communion table and stand reverently behind them. The pastor continues the invitation, noting carefully the different ways you can "join church." One can join *by letter, Christian experience,* or as *a candidate for baptism.*

Joining church *by letter* means that you were a member in good standing of another church (preferably a sister church, but in most cases that does not matter). Those who come on *Christian experience* are Christians who have temporarily stepped away from the church for one reason or another; they are in reality "rejoining church." *Candidates for baptism* come as brand new Christians; yes, these brave souls are "joining church" for the first time in their lives, and therefore they need to be baptized. Once someone comes forward and takes one of those seats, the church clerk then moves into position, prepared to take down their information. Such was the experience of this brave young soul who would never back down from a dare.

My cousin, who was in town visiting, dared me to go forward and join. After the dare was made, and it was clearly understood by all parties involved, the next thing I knew I was sitting down in one of those seats in front of the church giving my information to the church clerk.

She did not ask me how I was going to "join church." Being so young (approximately ten years old) and having parents who were faithful members, she knew I was a candidate for baptism. I think I was the only one that Sunday to join church. So the pastor quickly made his way over to me, and as he took my hand he asked the church clerk for her report, then proceeded to the Q&A. This of course was all perfunctory because everyone in the church knew what the pastor would ask and how I would answer. He asked if I wanted to join church and get baptized, and of course I answered both questions in the affirmative. All baptizing was done immediately following worship on the first Sunday of the coming month. This was followed by a communion service that same evening when all who joined church that prior month would receive the "right hand of fellowship" entitling them to "all the rights and privileges of any member of the church." Although I did not understand these phrases, there was something attractive about them. Even though I had been dared, something deep inside of me wanted to join church and receive "the right hand of fellowship" and have "all the rights and privileges of any member of the church." So I was glad and even proud that on that particular Sunday when "the doors of the church were opened," I in my mind felt that I had walked in.

Why Do They Bring Their Bibles to Church?

Several years passed and I, like all the other youth, was highly involved in church work. You would spot me in Sunday school, the Sunshine Band (little kids choir), Junior Usher Board (I was pretty good at this), Baptist Training Union (BTU), youth choir, softball team (I was awesome at this), and the Youth Council (youth group).

My parents were good church workers. My father worked faithfully with the youth of the church, especially the Junior Ushers. My mother sang in the adult choir and was a great cook. Her culinary skills earned her the role of chairperson of the kitchen committee. Therefore, since my parents were such diligent workers, we were at all of the church functions, dinners, and Sunday afternoon and evening programs. It was not unusual for the Love family to be at the church several times a week. For example, every department of the church had an anniversary or annual day. The choir (three of them), Usher Board (two of them), pastor, and church anniversaries took up a lot of time. We would invite other churches in the city to all of our activities, and in turn they would invite us to theirs. This meant that almost every Sunday we were either involved in one of our own annual days or participating as a guest at some other church, sometimes in the same city and often at a location requiring several hours of travel. This made for busy Sundays and busy weeks—all in the name of church work. Such was our life as a family, and for the most part we loved it.

You would think that with all that involvement in church activities, we as a family would be pretty good Bible students. Unfortunately, that was not the case. As a matter of fact, nothing could be farther from the truth. I recall only one man, Brother Alfred Bolden, who cared passionately about the Bible, and most kids and many adults considered him to be weird. The different programs and annual days got all of the attention.

The teaching departments of the church were marginalized. Sunday school, BTU, and Wednesday night Bible study always took a backseat to the "programs." We were a busy church, and we enjoyed the fellowship, but our church did not emphasize the study of the Bible (except for Brother Bolden, whom I now know was "a man of Issachar," a man who understood the times and knew what we should have been doing [1 Chron. 12:32]).

127

When Brother and Sister Lewis started coming to our church and bringing their Bibles with them all the time, you can imagine the stir it caused. They seemed to be nice people; they just had this strange attachment to their Bibles. Whenever you saw them, no matter what the church occasion, they had their Bibles with them. They also had a particular affinity for the church Bible study programs, and they would encourage our involvement in them.

They were even instrumental in starting for our church a week-long summer Bible study for young people (vacation Bible school). I was particularly fond of vacation Bible school because Brother Lewis let me drive his nice station wagon to pick up people, and Sister Lewis brought along her fine little sister, Jamie, who two years later would become my wife.

I found out later that they had come from what was called a "Fundamental Baptist church," where the preaching and teaching of the Bible were the most important activities (in contrast to our church with its many musicals and anniversaries). Brother and Sister Lewis were the first Christians to introduce me to phrases like "being saved" and "Jesus dying on the cross for my sins" and "asking Jesus to come into my heart." It was Sister Lewis who first taught me about "eternal security." When she asked if I thought people could lose their salvation, I had no idea what she was talking about. I did not know what salvation was or if I had it, so I did not give much thought to losing it. She explained that once Jesus saves you, you can never be lost again. All this new Bible stuff was kind of exciting and somewhat scary. I had never given much thought to what it meant to be saved or lost. My family and I went to church, we worked in church, and I had already been baptized and had received the right hand of fellowship, and that was all I felt was necessary. So when Sister Lewis taught me that there was much more to being a Christian than just being baptized or even "joining church," I was kind of intrigued, especially when she explained that one needed "a personal relationship with Jesus."

Now, I did not know about all that "saved stuff" or "asking Jesus to come into my heart," but I was sure of one thing: I did not have a personal relationship with Jesus. As a matter of fact, I had not really given much thought to Jesus up to this time. My knowledge of Jesus was scant at best, and this was unsettling to me. The notion of going to hell did not really move me. But the idea of not knowing Jesus left me feeling that even though I had just met the girl of my dreams, something in my life was not quite right.

One night after a long walk home from Jamie's house, I had what was probably my first heart-to-heart talk with Jesus. I said to him, "Lord, I am not sure if I have ever asked you to come into my heart and save me, and if I have not, I am asking you to do that now. Forgive me of my sins and be my Savior. In Jesus' Name, Amen." It was from this point that I began to consider myself a Christian, whether my life matched up to it or not (and in most cases it did not). But no worries, I was eternally secure—so I thought.

Now That Is the Kind of Preaching I Want to Do!

The next year, I sensed a call to preach, just like so many of the young "churchgoing" brothers in South Bend, Indiana. I do not think that my announcement came as a surprise to anyone, because I was faithful in church. So when the day arrived for me to preach my first sermon, excitement was everywhere. Preaching seemed to come naturally to me, because speaking in front of people did not bother me too much and because most of the preaching that I had heard did not seem to require too much effort.

Looking back on that first sermon, I realized that I made a real hash of James 1:1–2, but no problem—I knew I was going to get better as soon as I developed my own personal whoop.

My attitude about preaching completely changed when Pastor Robert Crockett Jr. visited our church as a guest preacher from Chicago (thanks to Brother Lewis). He was a Fundamental Baptist preacher with a Scripture recall that was absolutely phenomenal.

129

That Sunday pastor Crockett preached on Romans 1:16, and I remember his last point vividly: the person of the gospel. It was then that he quoted from memory Luke 1:1–20. The message was riveting; the clarity of Scripture was displayed in a way that I had never heard before.

I noticed that although they were not being fed much, our people did listen to the preacher. He commanded the congregation's attention every Sunday for forty-five to fifty minutes, and if he could get it right, I sensed that the impact would be phenomenal.

Pastor Crockett's passion was reverent and sincere, nothing like the entertainment driven preaching that I had grown up under. When he finished, I said in my heart, *Now that is the kind of preaching I want to do*. However, that kind of preaching would require much study. So I began to invest in tools. Brother Lewis introduced me to *Vine's Complete Expository Dictionary of Old and New Testament Words*, and early Saturday mornings he led me through the pastoral epistles. Another brother taught me how to use *Strong's Exhaustive Concordance of the Bible* with the Hebrew and Greek dictionaries. Listening to Christian radio I was introduced to preachers like John MacArthur, Charles Swindoll, Charles Stanley, and the late Vernon McGee.

Taking in a daily dose from these men kept my passion for the right kind of preaching alive, but it was Pastor Crockett whom the Lord used in my life to cause me to strive for excellence in the pulpit. He is still preaching at eighty-four years old, and I still want to preach like him.

This Just Ain't Getting It

Brother and Sister Lewis were also responsible for my hearing other great solid African-American preachers. Every year they would take me and my wife Jamie to the Abundant Life Crusade.

At these crusades, for the first time in my life, I heard several African-American men preach the Word of God minus the theatrics that had been passed off as good black preaching. At these Crusades preaching was the thing, surprisingly—not the offering, the choir, or all the "shoutin'" (emotions on overload). The preaching of the Word of God was the central activity. Our hearts would rejoice at the no-nonsense proclamation of the Word. When we returned to the whooping, hollering, rhythm and rhymes, no-Bible preaching tradition of our childhood, the letdown was sometimes beyond description. Our souls longed for much more. We left the church that I had grown up in, got baptized in, received the right hand of fellowship in, acknowledged my call to ministry in, got married in, and had our first child blessed in. The transition for Jamie and me was sometimes unbearable. We were quickly ostracized and thought to be brainwashed. The doors of churches where I had preached around town were suddenly closed. However, while many thought we were on the path to Cultville, the Lord actually had us on the path to truth.

I Am Not Going to Some White Church!

My former pastor was well connected in South Bend so there was no chance that I would be accepted at any of the other Missionary Baptist churches in town—not that we had any desire to go to any of them. Consequently, one Sunday morning in late 1981 (with Jamie two months away from delivering our second child) we found ourselves for the first time in our lives without a church home. This was not a happy feeling. My feisty brother-in-law, Lamarr, who was home from Bible college, urged us to attend Heritage Baptist Church, the all-white church just around the corner from our house.

I made it very clear that I was not going to some white church, and Jamie concurred. Lamarr kept on insisting, and then he said the magic word: "But Louie, it is a *fundamental* church, and the pastor is probably sound." Hearing that it was a fundamental church sparked my interest. After all, what did we have to lose? It's not like we had a church home anyway.

Lamarr and I arrived at Heritage Baptist Church (the weather was too bad for Jamie to go), and it was as white as white could be. Lamarr and I were the only brothers in the house, and because we are both six feet tall and "broke down clean" (dressed very well), we stood out like two sore thumbs. Although I had listened to many sermons by John MacArthur and was comfortable with the way I thought white men preached, sitting in one of their worship services was a whole new ballgame, and I was not sure I wanted to play.

We made it through most of the service, and then it was time for the preaching. The pastor preached a very high level overview of Ephesians that was easy to understand and quite convicting. When he gave the invitation for folks to come forward and pray, I turned to ask Lamarr if he wanted to go forward—he was already halfway down the aisle. I quickly joined him at the front. We prayed together kneeling in the front of this white congregation. After the dismissal we were immediately surrounded by many of the congregation. The pastor waited patiently in line to greet us. We introduced ourselves, and before I knew it I was telling this man all my business, how we came to be at this church, how we left the other church, and my desire to learn to be a better preacher.

I really ran my mouth that morning.

My reason for so much openness is because of the way this man preached. He reminded me a lot of John MacArthur. As far as I was concerned, the preaching of the Word far outweighed the fact that this was a white congregation and that the pastor was white. But could I convince Jamie of the same?

Jamie loved the Bible, and I knew that. Yet, like me, she was hesitant about attending a white congregation. Even so, Jamie took me at my word about the preacher, and she agreed to go and at least hear the man. The worship time was much different than we were accustomed to. The singing really tested our sanctification and commitment. They had no uniformed ushers, and nobody gave the announcements. This was more than unusual. Yet the preaching was on point, and we agreed that although it would be really tough, for now this was the place we should be.

The First Church

After several years at Heritage Baptist, we became restless. Though our understanding of the truth was limited, we still constantly thought about our black brothers and sisters who had no Bible knowledge at all. Eventually we left Heritage and moved to Dallas in order to attend Dallas Bible College so that I could learn the Bible and become a better preacher. After spending four years in Dallas and desiring the familiar ground of South Bend, we moved back home, and within a year I was called to my first pastorate. Wanting the people to really latch onto the Bible and evangelism, I began to preach a series through the book of Acts.

Fully armed with youthful exuberance and fundamental rigidity, I lasted a little over a year before the majority of the congregation had had enough. The vote came; I lost; and the church did the usual Missionary Baptist version of church planting—it split. I took some of the former members and planted another church. I was not as ready for this church as I was for the first one, and after a year, we left and moved to Chicago. Jamie landed a good job, we needed the fresh start, and although Illinois was never appealing to us before, right then it did not look so bad.

Two Strange-Sounding Preachers

Chicagoland seemed to have so much more to offer than South Bend, particularly better Christian radio. One morning while listening to Moody Radio, I heard a preacher with a funny accent. At first it was difficult to understand him, but I could tell he was rightly handling the Word. After a couple of days of listening to him, I finally caught on to his accent and learned that Alistair Begg was Scottish. It did not take long for Jamie and me to really come to appreciate this man's teaching. He had a way of communicating the Scripture that was compelling. We quickly began to accumulate his sermons on cassette tape.

I am an early riser. One day I turned on Christian radio, and there was another man with a rather raspy, peculiar sounding voice. I quickly learned his name was R. C. Sproul and wondered what he meant when he used the phrase *coram Deo*.

I introduced his teaching to Jamie, and we began to acquire his tapes, too. It was not long before I knew the meaning of *coram Deo* (Latin: before the face of God). I had no idea that the Lord was using these two men to introduce me to Reformed theology.

It should be understood at this point that I knew no theological categories like "Reformed," "Dispensationalism," "Calvinism," or "Arminianism." To me teaching was either sound or not. Sound meant that you could tell it was at least in the Bible and was in accord with the typical evangelical doctrines, such as divine inspiration of Scripture, the Trinity, and the deity of Christ.

I knew there was something peculiar about Alistair Begg's and R. C. Sproul's teaching, but I could not put my finger on it. I had taught through every book of the Bible several times, so it was not difficult to understand and accept what I heard from them and to square it with Scripture. What I loved about Begg and Sproul in particular was their emphasis on God. They often spoke of God's sovereignty, especially regarding salvation. My fundamentalist background led to a strong emphasis on man: there was always so much man was capable of and needed to do. I found out later that my view of man and his moral ability was rooted in Pelagianism.

Hacking My Way through Romans

Interestingly, I was first hit with TULIP, an acronym representing the doctrines of grace and also known as the five points of Calvinism, by a student at Dallas Theological Seminary. He ridiculed the whole notion of TULIP, and since I did not know what he was talking about, and since I had respect for him, I ignorantly laughed at TULIP as well.

The laughing stopped abruptly when I attempted to preach through the book of Romans. This should not have been that difficult of a task—after all, I had used the Roman Road numerous times in evangelism. It was business as usual, until I arrived at Romans 8, particularly verses 29–30:

> For those whom he foreknew he also predestined to be conformed to the image of his Son, in order that he might be the firstborn among many brothers. And those whom he predestined he also called, and those whom he called he also justified, and those whom he justified he also glorified.

I had read these verses many times and thought I understood them clearly. But this time they seemed to say something that I had not previously considered.

I had always understood foreknowledge to mean that God saw in the future that I would one day accept Christ, and therefore he elected me to be saved. However, that is not what these verses were saying. Upon studying these verses from a fresh point of view, I came to see that my salvation was totally up to God, and he arranged it all in advance. Then other passages of Scripture that I knew began to take on different meanings. I remembered that Ephesians said something similar. I jumped back to Romans and read on through chapter 9, and then that word appeared, the one that I unknowingly laughed at, the word that I had dismissed as a ridiculous man-made notion. It was right before my eyes in my Bible in Romans 9:11: "Though they were not yet born and had done nothing either good or bad—in order that God's purpose of *election* might continue, not because of works but because of him who calls." This changed everything. For years I had laid the full burden of salvation on man. I taught that with the right kind of techniques, powers of persuasion, or the right song for the invitation, man could be convinced that he needed to give his life to Jesus. Although I would pray for the salvation of family and friends, I still held that ultimately it was left to the decision-making power of the individual. So I became a rather efficient gospel salesman and could close the deal most of the time with people praying the prayer of salvation. After a few lines of "Just as I Am" and a good bleeding heart story, hands would go up all over the place. I did for the altar call what Tiger Woods did for golf.

Then in a moment all that I had believed and taught about salvation was turned on its head. Men, women, boys, and girls are saved not because they have been persuaded to choose God, but because God chose them before the foundation of the world. He elected them to salvation. I even had to rethink the implications of one of my favorite invitation songs, "I Have Decided to Follow Jesus."

My preaching and invitational system had left salvation entirely up to man; my gospel presentations made our Triune God simply a provider of a way of salvation, and the rest was up to man. Yes, the Father initiated the plan, Jesus provided the sacrifice, and the Holy Spirit would convict man of sin, but in the end it was left up to man to decided if what the Father, the Son, and the Holy Spirit had done was worthy of acceptance. So although I did not know I had theological categories, I indeed was teaching a theology—a bad theology.

Off to the Conferences

In May of 2001 I had my first opportunity to attend a pastor's conference. Parkside Church in Ohio had a conference for pastors hosted by Alistair Begg that had been on my list for over a year. Earlier that year I had heard Alistair in person for the first time at Moody Founder's Week. He was followed by a man named John Piper. Since I had not heard of John Piper, I left after Alistair was done.

The month of May could not come soon enough. Although Jamie did not attend the conference, she took the trip with me so that she could browse the bookstore. We both were amazed that Parkside bookstore had allotted an entire rack for that man named John Piper. Everything he had written was in abundance, and everyone seemed interested in his stuff. I was convinced that if Alistair had John Piper in his bookstore, then he must be worth reading. I picked up *God's Passion for His Glory*, and began to devour it. It should be no surprise that nine months later, in February 2002, I was front and center at Bethlehem Baptist Church's conference for pastors, hosted by John Piper.

John Piper was the first man I heard that used the phrase "Reformed theology" so freely. He told a story about how he had heard about a couple of Reformed African-American men who had a passion for bringing the truths of the Reformation to African-Americans: Sherard Burns and Anthony Carter. Burns was slated to be one of the speakers for the conference that year, and Carter preached in 2003. These two men guided me to officially embrace Reformed theology and to intentionally teach it to the church I pastored. However, there was one thing I noticed at Parkside's and Bethlehem's conferences: African-Americans were few in number. I soon discovered that Reformed theology was the least accepted theology among African-Americans. Bringing our people to embrace the historic teaching of the church would be no small order, but it needed to be attended to.

Bringing It Home

Since conferences were helpful for me, I decided to host one for our church and our area near Chicago. I decided to let Anthony Carter help me to bring these truths to our congregation and others in Lake County, Illinois.

To prepare the congregation for the conference, I encouraged the members to read James Montgomery Boice and Philip Graham Ryken's *The Doctrines of Grace: Rediscovering the Evangelical Gospel.* Reading the book and listening to the conference sessions with Carter led to the congregation gladly receiving and accepting the doctrines of grace.

The doctrines of grace, or TULIP, brought liveliness to our congregation—from the Bible studies to the worship. It is like we were set free from our "free wills." TULIP, which I had ridiculed many years before, was now almost a watchword as each member sought to memorize its doctrines.

The knowledge of God's sovereign grace in salvation that has set us free from the bondage of sin changed the way and manner of our corporate worship, especially the preaching. I was convinced from even my early days that preaching was to be the central activity in the corporate worship. My fundamentalist background usually led me to preach imperatives: "do this, do that." God's sovereign grace in salvation made me think more on the indicatives of Scripture. I was graciously forced to explain the work of our triune God in salvation. Old familiar passages, such as John 1:12, that were used in gospel presentations now needed to be explained along with John 1:13, which demonstrates the initiative of God in salvation.

The popular John 3:16 text had to be re-examined in light of knowing that regeneration is monergistic, which is a work of God alone. Preaching the gospel would have to change from "what you should do" to "this is what God has done." Biblical theology's emphasis on Christ as the subject of all the Scriptures and redemption being the thread throughout would now inform my exposition of Scripture. Just the thought of preaching Christ from the Old Testament is remarkable. No longer could chapters and books of the Bible be hijacked for the interest of the soapbox.

Old hymns such as "There Is a Fountain Filled with Blood" and "Amazing Grace," once sung without thought, took on new meaning. Songs of praise that celebrate the Father's planned salvation, the Son's accomplished salvation, and the Holy Spirit's application of salvation are now in demand. "Before the Throne of God Above," "In Christ Alone," and "I Know My Redeemer Lives," among others, have taken the place of the melancholy so-called Gospel songs that are so much of the African-American church tradition.

The changes we were going through as a congregation did not come without some casualties. But by God's grace we lost only one family because of our newly embraced theology.

Soteriology Was Just the Beginning

Although soteriology, the doctrine of salvation, was the entrance point for me to embrace Reformed theology, this was truly just the beginning. Many other theological considerations became open for scrutiny. This was my argument: if I had by default accepted a faulty understanding of the gospel, salvation, and the doctrine of the church, then maybe I needed to review all the major doctrines of the Bible. This is what I did and what I am still doing. Yet it all began with salvation—and this is the case with many African-Americans who are embracing the truths of the Reformation. Many have come from faulty understandings of the gospel, and when hearing the doctrines of grace, their hearts are set free. Was I truly a believer back in the day when I walked forward, took my seat, got baptized, and received the right hand of fellowship, obtaining all the rights and privileges of any other member of the church? Probably not. Was I truly "saved" when I asked Jesus in my heart on that peaceful weekday evening? I really don't know. However, as my mother used to say, "I know one thing"—when the Lord gripped my heart with the truth of his sovereign grace in salvation from the pages of the book of Romans, "the doors of the church were opened," and by God's amazing grace, I most assuredly walked in.

Now I say with the psalmist:

> Bless the LORD, O my soul,
>> and all that is within me,
>> bless his holy name!
> Bless the LORD, O my soul,
>> and forget not all his benefits,
> who forgives all your iniquity,
>> who heals all your diseases,
> who redeems your life from the pit,
>> who crowns you with steadfast love and mercy.
>> (Ps. 103:1–4)

Sovereign in a Sweet Home, School, and Solace

ERIC C. REDMOND

My introduction to Christ began as a child. Until I was a teen, I was raised in a nominally Christian, very moral, love-filled home. My parents, raised in the South, were churchgoers with a southern African-American, Judeo-Christian work, family, and community ethic. I was raised in the sort of home in which anyone would have wished to have been raised.

My parents emphasized the importance of an academically rigorous education, but they also enrolled my brother and me in local sports programs year-round. Weekends were filled with running from bowling to basketball tournaments to indoor soccer matches. In our high school years, every weekend was consumed with participation in a track meet. I am not sure how we managed to do it, but most Friday evenings for as long as I can remember, we seemed to have time for some chicken from "Roy's" (Roy Rogers) and a game of Scrabble. While my dietary limitations now give many chickens a sigh of relief, I still enjoy a challenge to Scrabble wherever and whenever anyone pulls out a board or online game.

Having grown up in the Civil Rights era, dad and mom faithfully instilled in their sons a sense of the importance of the history of African-Americans, giving us exposure to cultural, educational, and historical events associated with African-American life. We attended many Black History Month events, read the works of African-American authors, and participated in social events of African-American groups. Some of these events were sponsored by Delta Sigma Theta, my mother's sorority. Others were sponsored by Omega Psi Phi or a Prince Hall Masonic lodge of which my father was a member. Of great thrill annually was attending the jazz and Christmas concerts at the University of the District of Columbia, an HBCU where my father has served on faculty since 1970.[1] My family embraced the glories of African-American culture, and we enjoyed the richness of our history together. Or, as I like to say, I have sung my fair share of "We Shall Overcome" and "Lift Every Voice and Sing"!

Yet my parents also embraced diversity and the love of all people, such that I was able to take advantage of opportunities for exposure to the events, artifacts, literature, history, ideas, and ideals of broader American and Western cultures. Whether it was taking animation courses at the Corcoran Gallery of Art, enjoying an orchestral concert at the Kennedy Center for the Performing Arts, being sent to a leadership camp on the campus of St. Mary's College, participating in a college-prep science course at Johns Hopkins University, or playing soccer—sometimes as one of only two African-Americans on an all-white team—I was exposed to life that existed outside of African-American subculture. However, I was never allowed to forget that we were African-Americans.

Toward a Conversion

Prior to their conversions, quite often my parents responsibly took my brother and me to church with them on Sundays. On the Sundays they did not attend church, they placed my brother and me on the local Sunday school van of a Southern Baptist Convention church near our home. It was not a black church, but it was church, nonetheless. I can remember going to church as a regular Sunday occurrence (except when I was playing soccer, for soccer is a Sunday sport).

However, it was through the work of two missionaries appointed by the SBC Home Mission Board (now the North American Mission Board), who preached the gospel to us in the van every Sunday, that I was introduced to Christ as a child in my late-elementary/pre-teen years. I can remember reciting John 3:16 every Sunday in the van and in Sunday school class. I also remember the stories of Christ's work in the personal lives of the teachers and missionaries who so kindly shared Christ with the children from our neighborhood.

It was not until my parents experienced conversion by Christ that my home took on a distinctively Christian experience. By the mighty working of the Lord's grace, his work of sanctification in my parents has never diminished from the time of their commitments to Christ. Today they are two of the most mature and sincere believers I know.

Initiation into African-American Discipleship

The First Baptist Church of Highland Park in Landover, Maryland, is the church I call "home." It is an African-American assembly with membership in the Progressive National Baptist Convention (PNBC) and in the National Association for the Advancement of Colored People (NAACP). As a teenager, this was the first church where I joined as a member. It was there that I enjoyed the best of African-American church culture. I heard fiery sermons appropriated to African-American life, especially during the annual spring or fall revivals when nationally known preachers from around the PNBC world came to our pulpit. Occasionally we would hear a "whoop," "song," "squall," or "tune" at the end of a sermon. I can say for certain that I heard the gospel preached from that pulpit in its simplest form, even if all of the implications were not drawn out week to week.

I also enjoyed great music and singing in the African-American tradition at "the Park" (as it is affectionately known). We could shout, clap, sway, and sing with the best in African-American tradition. So full on each service was the amount of music (and unfortunately, the number of announcements!), that corporate worship ran at least two and one-half hours every Sunday. But we were enjoying ourselves, and since this was all we knew as church, no one became restless from the length of the service. Even if you did as a child, you got the church pinch from your mother, which was more of her nails being driven into your thigh or forearm to remind you to be still and quiet, *or else*. I avoided the "or else," but not the pinches, and I probably still have scars in my thighs to prove it.

The Park is where I served as a young adult usher, so I learned to appreciate standing in the aisle with one hand behind my back and marching around for the offering period on special occasions. It is also the place where I gained my first experiences in sharing my faith, speaking on youth Sundays, visiting the sick, listening to mothers in the church cry out to "Lord Jesus" and "Master" with long prayers from the depths of their souls, and watching deacons serve the Lord's Supper and govern the workings of the church with (and sometimes, very wrongly, *over*) the pastor. Even though the Park had central air conditioning, on packed summer days we waved fans (from the local funeral home) with Martin Luther King Jr.'s picture on the front. *Home* is where I saw deaconesses dressed in black on second Sundays, the missionaries dressed in white on fifth Sundays (albeit a different white than nurses and the ushers), and each choir dressed in different-colored robes.

Most significantly, the Park had a strong emphasis on classroom Bible teaching, through the PNBC Congress of Christian Education, the local minister's conference, and the continuing education program at nearby Washington Bible College in Lanham, Maryland. Because the Park emphasized teaching and studying the Scriptures, it was through this church of people of African-American heritage and descent that the Lord prepared my heart for studies in the Scripture that would change how I viewed church and the world forever. For through one of those courses, I would become a Bible college student—with my church's blessing.

Studying the Scriptures in a formal academic setting was an incredible experience for me as a young adult! I learned things that I never learned in Sunday school or from the pulpit, and I learned at a depth unparalleled by anything I had previously encountered, even on Christian radio. One of the things that contributed to such intense and thorough learning was the rigorous debates we students were able to have. Fortunately for me, a controversial debate arose in my first semester of school over a newly published book called *The Gospel According to Jesus*.[2] I received a copy of this book for Christmas of that year and read it voraciously.

Introduction to Reformed Theology

John MacArthur, I would soon learn, has never been one to mince words, water down the truth, or back down from a controversy—an example I appreciate to this day. As the author of *The Gospel According to Jesus*, his no-nonsense approach to clarifying the gospel that should be taught from every pulpit forced me to think about what I believed about conversion and discipleship. While the debate seemed to center around "cheap grace" and "easy-believism," I found the issues in the book to be very simple: *what is the message of the gospel, and what does true belief look like?*

For MacArthur, the gospel could be explained by Reformed theology's emphasis on the sovereignty of God:

> We must remember above all that salvation is a sovereign work of God. Biblically it is defined by what it produces, not by what one does to get it. Works are *not* necessary to earn salvation. But true salvation wrought by God will not fail to produce the good works that are its fruit (cf. Matthew 7:17). We are God's workmanship. No aspect of salvation is merited by human works (Titus 3:5–7). Thus salvation cannot be defective in any dimension. As a part of His saving work, God will produce repentance, faith, sanctification,

yieldedness, obedience, and ultimately glorification. Since he is not dependent on human effort in producing those elements, an experience that lacks any of them cannot be the saving work of God.[3]

The Gospel According to Jesus helped me understand why it was that I saw biblical faith being lived out only by a handful of people I loved and admired among the congregation I knew as my church family. A lack of transformation in moral thinking and an acceptance of low standards for purity were related to the gospel that was being (or not being) preached from our pulpit. Little accountability for growth in the Scriptures, in which personal or group study was entirely optional, was tied to disjointed messages as food for the sheep. There was no systematic tying of the sovereign God's rule over all to his rule in calling us to faith and keeping his own victoriously in the faith. Because MacArthur was clear on what the Scriptures taught about the gospel and conversion, I dared to ask myself: Are many of the people I love actually *saved*? If so, why is growth in the faith, other than developing nice manners, minimally visible? Why do so few continue in what appears to be faith when they leave for college? Why does faith seem to have no affect on who we are as African-Americans, such that we talk, work, spend, view television, educate ourselves, raise children, consider moral issues, and relate in marriage just like all other African-Americans—even those who have no faith in Christ? In reading the Scriptures with an understanding of Reformed theology, I began to find answers to these questions that were consistent with the picture of the promise and expected working of the gospel in the Scriptures.[4]

As a young adult, I was not completely sold by MacArthur's arguments for every aspect of Reformed theology, but I had no reason to disagree. Even so, I did not yet understand all the implications of a correct understanding of the gospel for church ministry and the work of evangelism. Fortunately for me, another student told me that I could get a student subscription (read "free subscription") to *Tabletalk*, a devotional journal from Ligonier Ministries. While I disagreed with much of *Tabletalk's* teaching on eschatology, I learned to embrace its teachings about the essence of the gospel and a persevering faith. Even so, after three years of learning Bible and theology and reading *Tabletalk* and academic journals, I still needed one more resource to help me fully understand what I was coming to comprehend.

A Godward Awakening

In the fall of 1991, I came to a sort of crisis of understanding.[5] I had been overloaded with truth in my three years of schooling. I had been given opportunities to teach adults the Scriptures, to share my faith on the street, to visit the sick, and I had started preaching—or more appropriately *I answered the call to preach and was licensed to the gospel ministry!* However, I could not figure out how this knowledge related to all of life. I knew I was to carry out the Great Commission. I knew I was to love my wife, preach the Scriptures expositionally, and serve faithfully. *But there must be something more,* I thought to myself.

One night, after voicing my crisis to my wife, Pam, we thought that a trip to the bookstore might be good. Since I enjoyed reading, maybe I could find something there that would be helpful. As the Almighty would have it—as he *decreed* I would later learn—a book with an interesting term in the title caught my eye: *Desiring God: Meditations of a Christian Hedonist.* I thought, *What in the world is a* Christian *Hedonist?* I had to know.

It would not be a stretch to say that reading John Piper's *Desiring God* changed my life. I could not put the book down! (I have heard that many have shared such an experience.) Finally, I had learned the inherent truth of the gospel that united all of life, the cross, and the resurrection: God wants me to glorify him by enjoying him forever in every area of my life. And here was a book that explained how to enjoy God in worship, prayer, the Scriptures, marriage, work, missions, suffering, and finances! A Christian hedonist was born! I wanted to "delight myself in the Lord" as a way of life!

Seeing Reformed theology as Christian hedonism—the joy of God on every page of Scripture and in all of life—gave me a reason for everything I did henceforth. I was to teach in order to help open the eyes of believers to the happy God.[6] I was to share my faith so that others might delight themselves in the Lord.[7] I was to love my wife that I might have my joy in the joy of my beloved.[8] I began to fight against gritting my teeth while serving, but instead counting all things joy while serving.[9] Christian hedonism led to a personal Christian enlightenment and reformation for me. Equally as important to my experience was that Christian hedonism pointed me to the Reformed faith. What do I mean by this?

In *Desiring God*, Piper alludes to the Westminster Shorter Catechism as a partial framework for the simple statement of Christian hedonism: "What is the chief end of man? Man's chief end is to glorify God and enjoy him forever."[10] Having been taught from an early age to look up terms I did not understand, I had to learn about the Westminster Shorter Catechism. By God's grace, what I found is that the Westminster Shorter Catechism is one of the oldest tools for learning the Reformed faith. It is useful for studying systematically what one believes as a Christian.

Moreover, *Desiring God* introduced me to two other important tools of growth in my faith: other works by John Piper and the works of Jonathan Edwards. In fact, the "wow" experience that I had when reading *Desiring God* seems only like a static shock compared to what I felt after reading *The Pleasures of God* and books on the life and teachings of Edwards.[11] Now I was having "aha" experiences that were more like nuclear reactions! How could I have previously missed that God works to secure the salvation of the elect in such a way that it pleased the Lord to bruise Christ on the cross?[12] How could I have missed that the Trinity never changed in its happy, holy delight—even being full of joy—as a Father killed his own Son for us?[13] Why hadn't I heard before that chief end and ultimate end were one, and that those ends were his glory? Even as I relive these moments of awakening through this writing, I can hardly contain my joy! The truths of Reformed theology have been a deep well and flowing river of satisfied desire for me.[14]

A Theology for Whites Only

Having portrayed MacArthur, Sproul, Piper, and Edwards as my heroes, I feel that I must answer the oft-spoken charge, "Isn't Reformed theology just for a bunch of (dead) white guys?" I suppose this is a fair question, since nearly everyone identified with the Protestant Reformation has been of European descent. But I suspect that this charge is not about history as much as it is about a modern identity. So let me explain how I have wrestled through the Christian version of the Uncle Tom epithet.

First, as African-American believers, we do have a history, and it started in Africa.[15] In our earliest history, in seems that we have record only of Lemuel Hayes as being radically Reformed in his theology[16] However, there are others we can point to in African-American history who confessed Christ and preached of him. But they lived in Africa or America, not Germany, France, Switzerland, Great Britain, or Ireland, and some of them were traveling in chains from West Africa to the East Coast of the United States during the time of Puritanism. So we do not hear of them among the Reformers and Puritans. Yet they do exist in our history.

Second, we must recognize that there is something more to race than one's philosophy about race. African-Americans have endured and continue to experience racism, bigotry, prejudice, and discrimination because our skin color(s) and folkways differ from people of European descent, not because of an ideology. The nationalistic, isolationist, victimization, oppression, and dissimilation ideology common to African-American culture developed in the context of surviving mistreatment due to skin and folkways differences—much of that treatment stemming from ignorance about our people.

We are black—of African origin—and that never changes. So when we embrace Reformed theology, we do so inside this blackness, just as we do all of life in America behind Dubois's "veil."[17] However, one does not have to be philosophically or ideologically black in order to embrace or reject Reformed theology. Nor does one need to be of African origin to work to uplift African-Americans, for one should be concerned about all people no matter what their color. We know this because some abolitionists were of European descent. One does not lose one's skin color, folkways, or ideology when embracing Reformed theology, except where anyone's ideology contradicts the truth of Scripture. I strive for the uplifting of our people, but I do so in grace through the preaching of the gospel and the reformation of our churches.

If a person would allow himself to be pigeonholed into becoming a person of a nationalistic or ethnocentric thought out of the fear of being viewed as an Oreo or Uncle Tom, then Reformed theology is not for that person. But then neither is the gospel, for the gospel calls each of us to stand against an ethnic-centered philosophy of one's own race, for such a philosophy is naturally conformed to this present world and is in need of redemption. If you cannot stand against your own culture where it does not square with the Scriptures, you are the one who is ashamed of Christ, and such shame has nothing to do with philosophical or ontological blackness; it only has to do with your view of the majesty of the God who calls you to deny yourself in order to follow Christ.

The Origin of Racism

With all that being said, one still might need to wrestle through a mischaracterization of Reformed theology in general and of the biblical teaching on *election* (or predestination) in particular. I have written elsewhere on this; my ordination council raised this issue as a problem it had with Reformed theology:

> I appeared before an ordination council comprised of African-American ministers, only one of which could be identified as "evangelical." During the council, one of the points on which I received the greatest challenge was my belief in the doctrine of election. "So you believe in predestination," said the most hostile council member with disdain in his voice. "Yes," I replied unashamedly. "But don't you know . . ." he began to retort, but I cut him off, saying, "that predestination was used by antebellum slave masters to propagate slavery? Yes, but that was a misuse of the Scriptures." But the council member angrily continued, "but don't you know that belief in predestination is the basis for this country's racism?"[18]

150

The sentiment expressed by the member of my ordination council is commonly felt by African-Americans. It is one of the ills left from the antebellum period of our history that is still poisoning our people against the precious truth of God's sovereignty in election. For example, if God decreed African-Americans to be slaves, and slavery was an injustice to the slaves, then God is unjust. If God is unjust, I do not wish to serve him. Therefore—so the reasoning continues—God could not be unjust, therefore God could not have (approvingly) decreed African-Americans to be slaves. Therefore there is no such thing as predestination or a God who predestines, and therefore Reformed theology is categorically dismissed.

It is beyond the scope of the story of my journey to address the logical fallacies in the above reasoning.[19] Many others have sufficiently addressed the issue of God's love in election.[20] Nevertheless, in order to help one reason his way to Reformed theology from the gross injustices African-Americans have experienced under the hand of an absolute God and a Sovereign God—one who is sovereign over racism too—I must ask the following: *What has spawned liberal theology, health and wealth theology, and the absence of men in our churches?* Rather than the vibrant teaching of the sovereign rule of God, is it not the Pelagian and Arminian beliefs consistently fed to people from our pulpits for the last century (or at least since the end of the Civil Rights era)? Will Reformed theology be faulted for the present social and moral status of our community?

As a dreamer, I like to think of what might have happened if our pulpits had preached Reformed theology and its implications for living over the last two generations. I suspect that the very social things we have desired could be achieved if God so chose to grant such grace as we await the second coming. For example, economic depression can be addressed by preaching about (1) the accountability of all men to be economically impartial,[21] (2) helping the needy as one of the chief ends of job employment,[22] (3) the responsibility of the body of Christ to care for its own,[23] (4) the need for contentment as a spiritual discipline before the God who supplies all things,[24] (5) the ability to endure lean times by Christ's power,[25] (6) the rule of God over oppressive governments,[26] and (7) the call to invest earthly wealth toward the kingdom of heaven as those who worship God and not mammon.[27] Preaching that only focuses on what the government must do to provide economic justice does not consider the rule of Christ to fulfill empty, unfulfilled, and unsatisfied souls through the church through the gospel. The faithful Christ-centered preaching of Reformed theology considers God's lordship over all things.

As one who holds to the lordship of Christ in all things, I have come to recognize that he is sovereign in salvation. When I first heard the truth about election, I admit that I bristled. I had been so used to hearing the emphasis on the universal invitation of the gospel that I am not certain that I had ever heard the truth of election—that God has freely and mercifully chosen whom he will save, that this is the only way anyone is ever saved, and that only those chosen will be saved.

Seriously considering Scripture's description of how radically and utterly depraved we are as people before a holy God helped my understanding. Scripture depicts each of us as sinners by both nature and actions, as people who are spiritually blind, ignorant of God, hard-hearted toward God, without hope, suppressors of the truth about God, and as people who prefer warped formations of the creation rather than God himself. We are not people who would naturally choose God; naturally we reject God and enjoy sin. I was able to see that without election, no one would ever be saved.

The Practical Importance of Reformed Theology

A God so sovereign that he can override rebellious hearts is a God in whom we can place our hopes, for nothing can thwart his will. He has power to do all things. One so sovereign that he overrides the selfish and rebellious wills of sinners in order to give them a heart that responds to him can override all selfishness and rebellion! I can now preach about a God who can stop a divorce and save a marriage in which emotional and erotic love has disappeared, while he holds the trusting believer's heart together. I can encourage people to trust the God who can turn the heart of an employer to grant a favorable evaluation or mercy when unearned time off from work is needed. Further, I can share my own testimony of how God can keep a family in peace through the darkest days of losing a child.

In 1995, four months into our third pregnancy, Pam and I were told that our unborn child had a birth defect that would lead to death within an hour of his birth. Over the following six weeks, we were repeatedly given the option of an abortion. But fearing the Author of life, and knowing that our God had the power to miraculously save the child or comfort us through his death, we kindly asked our medical team to stop asking us about the abortion option, for this is not an option for those who trust in the Lord.

Four months later, Eric C. Redmond Jr. came to us by stillbirth. It had to be the saddest moment of our young married lives. Over the next year we shed more tears over losing our son than we had shed over anything else. Enduring the last four months of gestation with the knowledge of the impending death was hard; not having a child to hold when many of our friends welcomed babies into their homes over the next year was even harder. It was painful to hear cries from others' babies when we should have heard cries coming out of our own arms. Yet we knew at that time that God was glorified before all with our obedience.

When you serve a sovereign God, there are so many ways in which he gains all glory from ruling in our trials. I suppose we will not know them all until we see him face to face. But this much I do know: over the next year, through the attention Pam and I gave to one another's pain, we drew even closer together in love in our marriage. Although we were one of only a few African-American families in membership at a large, predominantly white church, and we were only in our first year of membership, the church walked with us through the pain, and we developed friendships across racial lines—friendships that continue to this day as some of the most cherished ones we have. We had a miscarriage that next year, but God provided encouragement through our friendship and married love so that we were sustained through the pain on top of pain.

Two years after the stillbirth, thinking we could not have any more children, the Lord softened our hearts to consider adoption. While participating in the initial adoption session, we learned that we were pregnant. (We stopped the adoption process, but remained open to adoption.) Later that year, our third daughter was born, and she continues to be one of the most precious gifts ever given to two undeserving sinners.

Since the year of the stillbirth, we have been able to use that experience to encourage others who have experienced stillbirth or miscarriage and tell people that with our sovereign God's guidance, marriage can make it through any trial. I have been able to preach the pro-life message as one who has lived through a scenario that is often used to argue for the choice position—without choosing murder. We have seen the faithfulness of the sovereign God, and know that he can do the same for all under his good rule.

A Theology of Glory

Another blessing to our family has come from trusting God's rule in life and death. In 2004, still being open to adoption and still hoping for sons, we became adoptive parents (for which there is a great need in the African-American community). Christ the Lord placed two wonderful sons into our lives, for which we are most grateful. We are grateful to God for the sons themselves, but also for the way he ruled in our lives to make us open to adoption—while filling our joy through the pain of stillbirth.

For me, Reformed theology is not about theories to be disputed in the blogosphere. It is about a theology to be lived out in the real world—the only theology that can be lived out in truth with joy in a world awaiting redemption. I love my heritage as an African-American and my rearing in the black church. I do not intend to deny who God has made me to be, nor does Reformed theology require me to do so. Instead, I am able to worship a God who rules in kindness in, through, and over all things that make me an African-American and a Christian African-American. It is this God who has called me and any who are Reformed to his glory road. Reader, I invite you and all African-American believers to join me on this journey—to the glory of God alone.

10

Looking for Love in All the Wrong Places

ROGER SKEPPLE

Although it might seem strange to those who are still a part of the theological system from whence I have journeyed, I stand today within a theological rubric that has afforded me both a greater understanding and a greater appreciation of the love of God. Throughout my journey, I have always heard that Reformed soteriology ignores the love of God, reduces it to an insignificant place, or belittles it. However, as I have found over the years, it is only in comprehending the elective love of God in the context of his righteous wrath against sin that we come to find and understand the true depth and extent of the love the Father has bestowed upon us in Christ. Truly I found love, albeit in all the wrong places (to some). How did I arrive at this place? Here is an account of my journey.

The Foundation of My Spiritual Awareness

My religious journey began off the shores of the United States on a small West Indian island known more for its beaches (365

155

in fact—a beach for every day of the year) than its theological heritage. It was there that I was born, and it was there that the religious framework in which I would be reared was set. Born into a family that was firmly nestled in the Pilgrim Holiness Church, we were methodistic in our doctrinal framework. But we were not just Methodists; I would later come to describe our family as intelligently and consistently Arminian. Both of my parents were school teachers and approached Scripture from not just an emotional and volitional vantage point, but an intellectual one as well. It would be several years, however, before I came to this realization.

While I was still a toddler, my parents moved our family from Antigua to North America in search of a greater level of opportunity for their three boys, I being the youngest. We moved to New York City, but that portion of our migration would be short-lived. When we arrived in 1966, the Civil Rights upheaval in the United States was in full swing. My parents made the decision to continue further north into Canada, where we settled. The cultural and social links to British society made that transition an easier one. However, being a deeply religious family, the cultural considerations could never supplant the religious ones, and my parents quickly searched for a spiritual home for their family. The lack of a church congruent to the Pilgrim Holiness Church, in which they were raised, led my parents to seek a strongly Wesleyan church that had beliefs that corresponded to it and in which they would be comfortable. We became a part of the Salvation Army.

Although many Christians only know of the Salvation Army as a social organization, it is a church whose history stretches back to the eighteen hundreds and the evangelistic work of William and Catherine Booth among the downtrodden of London's East End. I have strong memories of growing up Wesleyan and Holiness. Congregationally, worship was quite lively and spirited. Our church voiced a deep commitment to personal holiness, advocated a compassion for the needy and the hurting of society, and affirmed and practiced a commitment to individual ministry. But what was true of the congregation in general was more so in the case of our family. Daily family devotions in our home were as necessary and consistent as was our intake of food. My parents encouraged us from the time we were small to read the Scriptures and pray on our own. God was a regular part of our family experience, the most regular and essential part.

Spiritual Upheaval and Travail

Yet, in spite of all these things, I have to say that my years of spiritual awareness were also years of spiritual turmoil. Now, this should not have been the case, being that I experienced the best my spiritual heritage could have given to me. Could it be that it was not the heritage that was the issue, but the system itself? I would later discover that this was in fact the case.

The turmoil that marked my early years as a Wesleyan centered in a basic misconception of salvation, both as to how it was gained and how it was maintained. As to the former, while faith in Christ was advocated vigorously within our circles, an emphasis upon repentance as its contemporaneous consort was not. In this sense, sadly, we were squarely within the contextual framework of North American Christianity. We affirmed that the believer could by willfully sinning sever his relationship with Jesus Christ, resulting in the loss of his salvation, the typical Wesleyan position. This doctrine, combined with the Wesleyan belief that believers could attain a condition of entire sanctification, led to the conclusion in my mind that salvation was ultimately to be maintained by me.

The result of both of these doctrinal beliefs, as well as my misconceptions of them, led to some negative fallout in my growing spiritual awareness. For example, I could never attain a confidence regarding my spiritual relationship with God. Because I looked and waited for an experience that would usher in sanctification, the consistency of walking with God on a regular basis never materialized in my life. In my mind I would lose my salvation and then seek to gain it back on a regular basis. This further resulted in a life of spiritual hypocrisy, developed to mask the spiritual deficiencies that became more and more a pattern of my life.

From Hoops to Hope

Into this very confused life, God began to unravel the confusion and weave his order from a very unlikely place—basketball. Growing up, athletics was always an important part of my life. I played many sports in school, but I enjoyed none as much as I did basketball. Having grown up in Ontario, Canada, we had thirteen grades. At the end of my eleventh year, frustrated at my lack of playing time, I asked by parents if I could go to a basketball camp in Toronto. When my parents looked into this camp, they became concerned about the things they heard went on there during free time. They began searching for an alternative and came upon a Christian camp called Word of Life Youth Camp. My first response was very negative, but when they told me that Dr. J (Julius Erving) was going to be there, my attitude began to change. Little did I know just how life-altering that decision would be.

I know there is disagreement in some Christian circles as to the benefit that youth camps hold and what truly spiritual benefit can come out of them. However, I believe that my life would be much different today—for the worse—if not for the things that I learned there. Of all the things I walked away with from this camp in upstate New York, the most critical was an understanding that salvation was not something that could be lost, if it had been truly gained. I had never heard this before or seen it in the Scriptures, but I was completely captivated by it from the moment it was explained to me.

Having become convinced that salvation once truly received by faith could not be lost, I went home buoyed and jubilant that I could now be certain of my standing before God. However, there were many challenges I had to face. First, what I had learned was in disagreement with my church context. I wanted to and did tell all my peers of what I had learned and tried to convince them of the validity of my new understanding of salvation. While many noticed a positive difference in my spiritual temperature and perspective, the fact that I held a position with which my church disagreed meant many were apprehensive regarding what

I was advocating. My parents, the ones who knew me the best, had seen a change in me as well, but they too were excited and apprehensive. I was undaunted and continued to try to communicate what I had learned.

However, with spiritual advancement also came spiritual resistance and eventual failure. The system under which I had grown up proved to be more difficult to shed than just one week at a summer camp could accomplish. Only the groundwork was laid there; true lasting spiritual stability would take still more spiritual and biblical grounding.

What God Had Joined Together, I Had Put Asunder

A tremendously difficult aspect of the transition from Arminian theology to Reformed theology proved to be my emotional disposition. Still not fully understanding the complete soteriological underpinnings of my new belief, particularly the connection between justification and sanctification, my emotional state lagged behind my intellectual one, primarily because I had developed a pattern of projecting more than what I was actually living. In other words, I struggled with a life that was marked by hypocrisy. In many ways my experience mirrored that of H. A. Ironside, former pastor of Moody Church, who like myself was first exposed to the Holiness dogma and the perfectionism that is woven into it in the Salvation Army. In his book *The Vanishing Conscience*, John MacArthur wrote of Ironside's struggle and then quoted from one of his writings on this very matter:

> Ironside ultimately left the organization and abandoned his belief in perfectionism. He described perfectionism as a conscience-shattering doctrine:
>
>> The teaching of holiness in the flesh [perfectionism] tends to harden the conscience and to cause the one who professes it to lower the standard to his own poor experience. Any who move much among those in this profession will soon begin to realize how greatly prevalent are the conditions I have described. Holiness professors are frequently cutting,

censorious, uncharitable and harsh in their judgment of others. Exaggerations, amounting to downright dishonesty, are unconsciously encouraged by and often indulged in in their "testimony" meetings.[1]

The pattern of habitually living below my confession resulted in a sustained pattern of inconsistent Christian living. I easily slid back into some of the old mindsets related to salvation and sinful behavior, resulting in a continued struggle with the validity of my conversion.

The following summer again included a trip to Word of Life, and again I was exhorted to look at salvation aright and to stop seeking to base my salvation in myself and my own good works. But the old patterns of life and understanding seemed to constantly reassert themselves into my life. How would God bring me into a fuller understanding and experience of the truth? Again, God would use my parents and Word of Life.

Spiritual Boot Camp

In my final year of high school, I began to solidify my plans for the next phase of my life. I had always loved everything electric, both how they worked and what they did, so I planned to study to become an electrical engineer. Although my parents were totally behind my desires, they were also concerned as to whether I was spiritually prepared for life on a secular college campus. They saw weaknesses in my walk that I did not see. They were right. After some serious disagreement, I finally relented to their desire for me to attend a one-year Bible school before launching my engineer training. They allowed me, however, to choose the Bible school. I choose Word of Life Bible Institute, and that decision, as Robert Frost wrote, "has made all the difference." I went to Word of Life Bible Institute (WOLBI) a prideful young man, but left a humbled one; I went proud of what I would later find out was little more than biblical ignorance. I went spiritually incoherent; I left spiritually focused.

It is hard to imagine that one year could so change a life and one's direction in life, but such was the case for me. I cannot here describe the entire scope of what took place in my life through the ministry of WOLBI, but I hope just a few snapshots of that year will help convey its impact upon my life. One of the most life-molding experiences occurred the first week, when we were required to take a Bible knowledge test. I thought, having grown up in a Christian home, having read the Bible for years, having sat through every possible class offered at my local church, and having heard a multitude of sermons, I would show them just how much of the Bible I really knew. I still remember the answer sheet that went along with the test booklet. It contained several rows of multiple choice answers, of which I only completed one. I learned that day, very quickly, that I was completely ignorant of what was contained in the Scriptures and I desperately needed a Bible education. Although WOLBI never really told us why we took those tests, I think it was to demonstrate to all the "church kids" that they better listen to what was to be taught to them. Whatever the case, from that point forward I realized that to understand the Bible, I would have to do more than just read it, I would have to study it.

I learned that a personal, daily devotional life was an intricate part of a consistent Christian walk. Further, WOLBI taught me that leadership was as much about your example and life as anything else. Leaders lead by example and not by notifying everyone that they are leaders. At WOLBI I came to understand that living as a Christian in the world meant living a life that was different from those around you. That type of life took a commitment divorced from the need for applause, recognition, or acceptance by others. Two events stick out to me more than any others in this matter: my assignment in systematic theology and the events surrounding my call into the ministry.

The Word of Life curriculum was structured around Bible and theology. The Bible curriculum took place the first part of the school day and the theology curriculum the second part. I will come back to the Bible section in just a moment. I still do not know whether our theology teacher was a Calvinist, but it was through his instruction that I was introduced to a man named

John Calvin and a book that he had written called *Institutes of the Christian Religion.*

We had to write a paper for theology, and our work had to evidence research. One of the books in the library was the *Institutes*, and I remember reading through portions of it in my study. I do not remember the subject of that paper, written over a quarter of a century ago, but I remember my response to this day. I was shocked that there was a man who lived over four hundred years ago who believed similarly to myself, but so clearly articulated the Christian faith and salvation. I was hooked. From that time forward, Calvin would hold a special place in my pantheon of earthly heroes. God began to show me that the matter of not losing one's salvation was not some disparate teaching of the Scripture unhinged from other beliefs; rather, it was part of a marvelous system of theology taught in Scripture and articulated, humanly speaking, by those who adhered to the view of the Christian faith advocated by John Calvin. I knew little to nothing of the system or its history, but was convinced those aspects of it with which I was familiar were accurate biblically.

My Call to Full-Time Ministry

God was doing more with me than just honing my theology while at Bible school; he was also giving me a deep desire to see God's people taught the truth. I have to admit that as I began to understand the truth about the Christian faith, I also became steadily more dissatisfied with the form of Christianity under which I had been reared. Again, this was not because of a failure of my upbringing, for without the steady influence of my parents I would have been completely consumed by the evil all around and within me, but rather the failure of the system, the brand of Christianity under which I grew up. Yet, it was not the system that frustrated me the most. It was the lack of in-depth Bible teaching that fueled or sustained the system. And Bible instruction was a critical component of WOLBI. This would be critical in my call to full-time ministry.

The manner in which WOLBI conducted its Bible instruction was unique. Well-known evangelical Bible instructors came each week to instruct us on various books of the Bible. Coming from Canada and not being aware of the evangelical community in the United States, I had never heard of any of these individuals. Yet I was amazed week in and week out by the depth of biblical instruction to which each of these teachers took us. I realized that in-depth teaching of God's Word was the missing component to my life and the life of many people within my context.

As wonderful as this was, however, I quickly noticed something else about our instructors. They were all Caucasian. Having grown up in a white community, I was comfortable with people of any race, but I did begin to wonder if the black community in America had any in-depth Bible teachers. Again, I was unfamiliar with the United States. So, I began praying that God would raise up great teachers of his Word who were theologically sound within the black community. Little did I know that this prayer would begin to work in my own heart, and little did I know that the one black Bible instructor who came would have a strategic influence on my own development. His name was Dr. Tony Evans. It was at WOLBI where I first heard Dr. Evans speak, and I was convinced that in-depth Bible instruction in the black community was possible.

The more I prayed for God to raise up others, the more my own personal desires began to change from wanting to be an engineer to wanting to be a teacher of God's Word to God's people. Throughout my time at WOLBI, unique ministry and leadership opportunities were given to me, opportunities for which I did not ask, yet with which I was entrusted. As my time grew to a close there, the staff began to ask me if I would stay at Word of Life, come on staff, and continue my training for ministry. By now, I was convinced that full-time ministry was the direction in which I should head, so I was excited about the offer. My parents, however, would have some questions for me—as usual.

As educators, my parentes had a high opinion of educational endeavors and the benefit that such would afford to their children. They always lovingly pushed us to excel academically and supported us in our educational pursuits as much as a parent could. When I began sharing the administration's desire for me to stay on at Word of Life, while my parents were very excited for me, they asked me in several different ways if I believed I was properly prepared for ministry through my one year at the Bible Institute. I believed I was. However, what would I do later, if I wanted to move on from there? Would my education afford me sufficient opportunity? I had not really thought about that. As a nineteen-year-old, I was living in the moment. They also encouraged me that if Word of Life really wanted me to be a part of their organization, they should want me after I had finished my education. Convinced, I decided to transfer my credits and pursue a Bachelor's degree. But where would I go?

Most of the students graduating from WOLBI either went to Cedarville or to Liberty Baptist College (now Liberty University). I decided to apply to Liberty Baptist College and was accepted into their Bachelor's of Science program. Coming from Canada, all that my family had heard about Liberty and its controversial president, Dr. Jerry Falwell, was negative, especially their opinion of black people. So, with much fear and trepidation, I enrolled at Liberty in the fall of 1984. I transferred in as a junior because my thirteenth high school grade was counted as my freshman year and WOLBI gave me an incredible amount of Bible and theology hours. I was well on my way. My major was Pastoral Ministries and my minor was Biblical Studies. Liberty would prove to be another life-altering experience affecting every facet of my life.

A System and Not Just Beliefs

First, I met my wife, Teresa Hopkins, at Liberty. We would marry in 1987. She too was a transfer student (from Missouri), and we met where you would expect to meet your spouse—in Sociology class. However, this is a book about my journey to the Reformed faith, so I reluctantly move on.

The most instrumental events in my journey to the Reformed faith would take place in the classrooms and dormitories of this school. The reputation of WOLBI students preceded them to Liberty, and they were often identified immediately for various places of leadership. Such was the case with me, beginning as spiritual life director of my dorm. I would end up as a dorm supervisor the next year. I met various individuals of various theological backgrounds while there, including Arminians, three-point, four-point, and even some five-point Calvinists. Long, often emotionally charged debates over the theological intricacies of Scripture highly impacted my theological perspectives. I quickly learned that one cannot avoid certain Scriptures and scriptural issues. Your position is as strong as your weakest argument, and if you avoid certain passages and ideas, your opponent will press his case based on those weaknesses.

It was in the classrooms, however, that my theology and my approach to the Scriptures were solidified. Men such as Dr. Jim Freerksen and Dr. Neal Williams impressed upon me the need to understand the original languages if I was to understand the Scriptures fully. Through their ministry to me as my instructors (and Dr. Freerksen as my mentor), I committed myself to the study of the original languages of the Bible. Later, in seminary, I chose to major in Greek. My passion for background studies in large part grew from the influence of Dr. Williams, a master of several languages and an excellent Old Testament professor. But, of all my teachers, no instructor had as much an influence on me biblically or theologically as Dr. Paul Fink, head of the Bible Exposition Department at Liberty. Dr. Fink's approach to Scripture and to the ministry of preaching and teaching is the approach that undergirds and drives me to this very day.

The gifts that Dr. Fink gave me are innumerable. He gave me a love for the historical-grammatical method, a love affair I have maintained to this day. He taught me how to diagram sentences, both in English and in the original languages, which I still practice religiously. He taught me how to manuscript my sermons and preach from a manuscript in an engaging fashion, which defines how I currently preach. But of all the things that I learned from Dr. Fink, most crucial was the grand scheme of the Scriptures that the Calvinistic viewpoint teaches. Through his instruction I came to realize that there is a larger picture to Reformed doctrine—other than just salvation. I learned that history itself is under the lordship of Christ—telling his story, designed to illuminate his glory. Even before I came to know the meta-narrative system of understanding Scripture, Dr. Fink taught me to see everything—salvation, the kingdom, or any other major idea in Scripture—as being subservient to this one thing, namely, the glory of God. Yes, I was richly impacted by his ministry. I had come to Liberty with Calvinistic leanings; I would leave with a rooted Calvinistic self-awareness.

It's All Greek to Me

While at Liberty, my passion for pastoral ministry had begun to wane, and I sensed a longing to teach and train; at the time, I believed this was God's way of redirecting of my life into the work of a seminary professor. I excelled at Liberty academically. I graduated Magna Cum Laude and was also given the leadership award from the School of Religion. As I was accepting the award at a special award ceremony, Dr. Falwell asked me if I would be staying on at Liberty to continue my seminary training. Although I had already begun taking some seminary level courses before I graduated, I had not yet decided where I would attend seminary, but I was leaning toward Grace Theological Seminary. That many of my most proficient teachers of the languages and systematic theology came from Dallas Theological Seminary (DTS) was not lost on me, and I would have loved to attend there, however I did not believe I was academically fit to do so. One day, Dr. Williams, who was always interested in my work as a student, asked what my plans were. I told him about Grace. While he thought it was a good choice, he said based on my academic proficiencies he believed I should apply to DTS. I applied based on his counsel, and to my joy I was accepted.

Upon graduation Teresa and I were married, and after spending the summer living in Canada, we moved to Dallas so that I could start my seminary training. My desire in attending seminary was to master all the subject areas of biblical studies. Systematic theology was my first love, but I had read that B. B. Warfield, Charles Hodge, and A. A. Hodge were all Greek scholars before they turned to Systematics, so I decided to follow a similar path. For that reason I chose a double major at DTS: Systematic Theology and New Testament Literature and Exegesis. This allowed me to focus on my two loves, theology and Greek. I also took extra courses in all the other areas of biblical studies, allowing me to gain a comprehensive understanding of the background and contextual framework of the Holy Scriptures.

My primary purpose in attending DTS, however, was for the training in the original languages I would receive. I knew that the Reformed flavor of DTS had regressed by the time I began attending there in 1987. Although I disagreed with some of my professors' theological bent, I was always challenged in my beliefs, which was what I wanted. In fact, oftentimes I took classes in which I knew my beliefs differed so that I could learn how to defend what I believed from the strongest possible refutations of my position. Again, I believed that one's beliefs are best defended from one's weakest passages and ideas. If they can stand in that context, they can stand in any context. However, a number of my professors were definitely Calvinistic and reformational in their theology. Men such as John Hannah, Fredrick Howe, Wayne House, and Ken Sarles were unashamedly so, and I found them extremely encouraging in my continued journey to a fuller and clearer understanding of Reformed theology.

Even though I threw myself particularly into my language studies, I presented my thesis in the area of Systematics at the end of my four years of study. My thesis was entitled *A Moral Paradigm for the Freedom of the Will*. My reader coined a phrase to describe my approach to theology as "an exegetical systematic." It was through my work at Dallas Seminary that my approach to the Scriptures, my exegetical systematic, was solidified. This would define both my study of the Scriptures as well as my exposition. I graduated from DTS with honors.

Cutting My Teeth in Spiritual Ministry

While I was enrolled at DTS, my wife and I attended Oak Cliff Bible Fellowship (OCBF), where Tony Evans was the cofounder and senior pastor. We had no doubt that this would be our home church while in Dallas. Dr. Evans had come yearly to the church in which Teresa had grown up, and of course I had heard him at WOLBI, and later at Liberty as well. When we arrived in Dallas, we immediately joined the fellowship and began faithfully attending church. Through an internship offered by The Urban Alternative, an arm of Dr. Evans's Ministry designed to train seminarians in local church ministry, I began serving at OCBF in 1989 under Larry Mercer, Associate Pastor of Christian Education. I would later be licensed and ordained there in 1991.

Dr. Mercer had a great impact upon my life as he trained me in pastoral ministry and service for the next four years. Dr. Mercer was and is a rare combination: an expert in administrative philosophy and practice, as well as a master in Christian education. Hearing him and watching him gave me the Masters in Education I never took at seminary. Much of my administrative abilities today are a direct result of having served under his tutelage.

Two years after beginning my internship, I came on staff as Adult Education Director, in which capacity I served for one year. When Pastor Mercer left OCBF in 1992, I became the interim Associate Pastor of Christian Education in 1993, and then in 1994 "Interim" was dropped, and I was became the Associate Pastor. I served in that capacity for the next four years.

My years at OCBF were formative for some other reasons as well. First, I became fully convinced of the fifth and final of the five points of Calvinism, *limited atonement*. I had always supported those who affirmed all five points, and I had also advocated a watered-down concept of limited atonement—that Christ's death was sufficient for all, but efficient for only the elect. In 1996 I had planned to attend a family reunion in my place of birth, Antigua. Before I went, Faith Missionary Baptist Church, a Calvinistic church on the island, asked me to prepare a conference. While studying and preparing for that conference, I became completely convinced of particular atonement in its complete, unwatered-down form.

The second important occurrence at OCBF was that I learned to work with and appreciate those with whom I differed. Oakcliff was not a Calvinistic church by any means. In fact, in many ways the leadership was very opposed to Calvinism. However, Oakcliff was a church committed to biblical instruction and Christian living. Dr. Evans welcomed me into the fold in spite of our differences and allowed me to flourish and grow as a teacher and a preacher while I was there. These lessons would serve me well throughout my future years of ministry and service.

Another important experience was my introduction to the historical writings of the Puritans. One of the books I read in seminary for pastoral ministry was *The Reformed Pastor* by Richard Baxter. As I became more acquainted with the Puritans, I became aware of the deep separation between Reformed spirituality and Arminian spirituality. I began to more fully comprehend that the two systems separated from each other on the matter of sanctification. Such books as William Guthrie's *Christian's Great Interest* and *The Doctrine of Repentance*; Thomas Brooks's *Heaven on Earth*; John Owen's *The Glory of Christ* and *Communion with God*; and Ralph Venning's *The Sinfulness of Sin* left a lasting impression upon my life.

Georgia on My Mind

While at OCBF, other things were going on in my life. I enrolled in the PhD program in Biblical Studies with a major in Greek at DTS. I continued along this path until I later left Dallas for Atlanta. I had also self-published four books, one of which would turn out to be a key catalyst in our eventual move to Atlanta. Our transition from Dallas to Atlanta was associated with the passing of my father from cancer in 1997. It was in the year of his death that I was invited to Atlanta to be the keynote speaker at Carver Bible College's Founder's Bible Conference, focusing on one of the books I had self-published. I accepted, not realizing that this decision would play a role in changing the direction of my life.

My wife and I had been considering moving on from OCBF for some time, but had not looked into it deeply. When I arrived in

Atlanta for the conference, my friend Robert Crummie, a fellow Dallas seminarian, former member of OCBF, and vice president of Carver Bible College, asked me to consider coming to Atlanta and teaching at Carver. I indicated to Robert that I desired to pastor, but would consider teaching on the side if I were able to pastor in Atlanta. He said that there were some open pulpits of conservative churches in Atlanta, and he would inquire on my behalf. Nothing really materialized, except the opportunity to meet a few people who had some influence in the area, and so we returned back to Dallas at the end of the week to continue ministry and service.

At the end of 1997, with my father struggling with liver cancer, we made our way home to Kingston, Ontario, to spend some time with him and my mother during the holidays. I talked with him just before we left on our journey to Kingston, but by the time we arrived in town, he was hospitalized and on life support. I would never talk with my father again; he passed away on Christmas morning 1997.

A lot of things went through my mind during those difficult days. However, one conversation my father and I had had stuck out in my mind. He had told me while in the midst of struggling with his cancer, "Roger, whatever you plan to do in ministry, you better get to doing it." A few days after my father passed, I called back to Dallas to check my voicemail at work. There was a message from the head of the deacon/trustee board of Berean Bible Baptist Church in Atlanta, Anthony Dixon, wanting me to consider candidating for the position of pastor. Apparently one of the members of the church had attended the conference and heard me speak. When my name came up, there was a positive response. I contacted him from Canada and arranged a time for us to talk when I returned to Dallas.

Through much prayer, soul searching, and counsel, we decided to avail ourselves to this process. I began several trips back and forth between Dallas and Atlanta, interviewing and preaching. On May 13, Berean voted to call me as its second pastor, and I accepted. I began preaching immediately on Sunday May 17,

1998. I flew back and forth between the two cities for the next three weeks until we moved to Atlanta in June 1998.

The challenges that Berean presented were great, but God was greater still. Although the vetting process had been thorough, there were differences between myself and Berean that either party had not fully analyzed. As the first year was coming to an end, some of these differences were beginning to become problematic. By 1999 they turned into full-fledged conflict, centering on the reality of studying eldership, which had been agreed upon before I had agreed to come to Berean, and the doctrines of grace. Berean began to shrink in size, and the board digressed into gridlock. What would happen? I decided that if needed, I would leave Berean in order to save her from splitting. But God had something else in mind.

Quite amazingly, at a church meeting organized to deal with these issues, the congregation made a decision to disband the board and to appoint a temporary one in its place to finish the study of eldership and make a presentation to the church after that study was completed. Depending upon the outcome of the study, of course, a new constitution would have to be written. The Temporary Leadership Advisory Council was appointed in May 2000 and presented a completely rewritten constitution built upon the foundation of biblical eldership in April 2001, which miraculously passed with over 95 percent of the church deciding to vote themselves out of power and to submit to the rule of elders. Elders were chosen at the end of 2001 and were voted in by the congregation in January 2002. While the transition from a deacon/trustee board to an elder board has not been trouble free, it has been a true joy.

Berean has not only embraced the reality of eldership, it has also embraced the reality of the doctrines of grace and the five *solas* of the Reformation as an expression of reformational heritage, as well as the theocentric and christocentric hubs about which Reformed theology rotates.

So ends my journey, for now, preaching and teaching God's people in Atlanta of the great God who loves us with an eternal love. Yes, my journey to the Reformed faith has been an interest-

171

ing one. It has involved twenty-five years of biblical study and reexamination of all I have believed. It has been helped along by great books of the past and great men of my present. I thank God for all of them. My prayer for others is that your journey to the Reformed faith would give you as sweet a taste of God's love as mine has given me.

Afterword

Black, Reformed, but Foremost Christian

ANTHONY J. CARTER

All of the men who graciously and honestly tell their story in this book have at least three things in common. One, we are black Americans. Two, we are Reformed preachers and theologians. And three (and foremost), we are Spirit-filled Christians. All of these are significant designations, and each speaks and gives meaning to our history, our present existence, and our hope of future glory. We believe that each of these is according to the sovereign grace of God, for which we believe ourselves eternal debtors. Yet, each could be explained further and put into its proper place. What do we mean when we say that we are black, Reformed, and Christian?

Being black. This means that we have a distinct, if at times bitter, experience. It means that our parents often drank of the waters of Marah in a land that flowed with milk and honey. It means our foreparents felt the lash of the whip and witnessed the horror of babies and loved ones cast down to the depths of unknown graves in an angry deep during the Middle Passage.

It means their sweat and blood were fertilizer for a land upon which they could labor and see but never own. It means being African-American. It means we are ever conscious of minority status. It means having a face but often no name. It means having a home, but sensing no country. It means having a voice to cry with, but not a voice to vote with. It means having to learn to sing a joyous song in a strange, foreign land. It means learning to live upon a God who is invisible and trusting his purposes, though they seemingly ripen slowly.

Being Reformed. This means that we have a heritage that transcends our skin and ethnicity. It means that the grace of God has appeared to us according to his good pleasure. It means we see our God as sovereign, omnipotent, holy, and right. It means we see our sin for what it is, heinous and worthy of death. And it means we see our Savior as sufficient, immutable, and altogether good. It means that our heroes are not only men like Frederick Douglas and Booker T. Washington, and but they are also and to some degree even more so Martin Luther and John Calvin. It means our legacy is seen from Lemuel Haynes to D. Martyn Lloyd-Jones. We understand that we have as much in common with Martin Luther as we do with Martin Luther King Jr. John Bunyan and John Marrant belong to us as much as do Abraham Kuyper and A. Philip Randolph. It means that we can look to J. Gresham Machen and listen to his ability to articulate the dangers of the sin of liberalism and yet question his inability to comprehend the dangers of the sin of racism. It means that we have solid, historical, and biblical grounds upon which to stand as we seek to be an instrument of God in spreading his righteousness, peace, and joy throughout the world. It means that our ideology is informed by our theology, which is Reformed, because what we are first and foremost is Christian.

Being Christian. This means that we are first and last children of God. It means when you see one of us, you see a black man. But when you hear one of us, you hear a Christian man. It means that Christ is our Lord. It means that we are daily seeking to understand our African-American experience in light of the lordship of Christ. It means that we are nothing apart from the grace of God, and that God has created us who we are—to live during the times in which we live that we might show forth his mercies, while he is daily conforming us to the image of his dear Son. It means that our service—yes, our worship and allegiance—is not first to the black cause, though noble it may be at times. It is not first to the Reformed cause, though grand it may appear to be. It means that our service is to Christ first and last, now and at all times. If we can serve Christ while sincerely serving an African-American cause, then let us do it. If we can serve Christ while promoting a Reformed agenda, then by all means let us do so. But if Christ is in conflict with the black cause or the Reformed agenda at any point or at any time, then may we have the courage to say, "Away with blackness and away with Reformedness—give us Jesus and Jesus only." It means that we must understand that Martin Luther King Jr. gave his life that we might vote, but Christ gave his life that we might live. Frederick Douglas gave his life that we might be free from slavery, but Christ gave his life that we might be free from slavery to sin and death.

We are black; there is no mistaking that. We are Reformed, and make no mistake about that. But these two distinctions have relevance only insofar as they are understood in light of the fact that *we are Christian.* C. H. Spurgeon said, "I am never ashamed to avow myself a Calvinist; I do not hesitate to take the name of Baptist; but if I am asked what my creed is, I reply, 'It is Jesus Christ.'"

We are proud to be Americans. We are equally proud to be African-American. We even more thank God that our theology is the biblically grounded, historically consistent theology of the Reformation. But if you ask us our faith, if you ask us our creed, if you want the sum of our lives: It is Jesus Christ. It is Jesus Christ.

We pray that it would be yours as well.

Soli Deo Gloria!

Appendix

A Reformed Theology Survey

The men who have related parts of their stories in this book understand that we did not get to where we are by ourselves. We have been helped and encouraged by books, family, friends, teachers, and preachers. We understand that God has used, and continues to use, various ways of encouraging us in our journeys. To this end, the following are answers to these questions asked of those who contributed to this book:

1. What was the first book you read that introduced you to Reformed theology?
2. Besides the Bible, list the five most influential books in your Reformed theological journey.
3. List three preachers and/or teachers who were most influential in your journey.
4. If you could give one book to someone interested in Reformed theology, what would you give them?

Reddit Andrews III

1. *Lectures to My Students*, C. H. Spurgeon
2. *Knowing God*, J. I. Packer; *Systematic Theology*, Louis Berkhof; *The Biography of D. Martyn Lloyd-Jones*, Iain Murray; *The Works of Jonathan Edwards*, Jonathan Edwards; *Our Reasonable Faith*, Herman Bavinck
3. LeRoy Bailey Jr., Gary Cohen, D. Martyn Lloyd-Jones, Allan Joseph
4. *Systematic Theology*, Louis Berkhof

Thabiti Anyabwile

1. *Knowing God*, J. I. Packer and *Great Doctrines of the Bible*, D. Martyn Lloyd-Jones
2. *Knowing God*, J. I. Packer; *Great Doctrines of the Bible*, D. Martyn Lloyd-Jones; *Bondage of the Will*, Martin Luther; *What Is Reformed Theology?* (previously *Grace Unknown*), R. C. Sproul; *Chosen but Free*, Norman Geisler (I read as a defense of the non-Reformed view. Its weaknesses pushed me more conclusively to a Reformed understanding.)
3. R. C. Sproul, John MacArthur, Mark Dever
4. *What Is Reformed Theology?* R. C. Sproul

Anthony B. Bradley

1. *Putting Amazing Back into Grace*, Michael S. Horton
2. *Institutes of the Christian Religion*, John Calvin; *Puritan Race Virtue, Vice, and Values 1620–1820*, Joseph R. Washington Jr.; *From Creation to Consummation*, Gerard Van Groningen; *Christ-Centered Preaching*, Bryan Chapell; *Van Til's Apologetics*, Greg L. Bahnsen
3. Cornelius Henderson, David C. Jones, Gerard Van Groningen
4. *Far as the Curse Is Found*, Michael D. Williams

Anthony J. Carter

1. *Knowing God*, J. I. Packer
2. *The Pilgrim's Progress*, John Bunyan; *Institutes of the Christian Religion*, John Calvin; *Knowing God*, J. I. Packer, *The Five Points of Calvinism*, David N. Steele and Curtis C. Thomas; *The Reformed Doctrine of Predestination*, Loraine Boettner
3. Ezra Ware, R. C. Sproul, Richard Pratt
4. *The Reformed Doctrine of Predestination*, Loraine Boettner

Ken Jones

1. *Institutes of the Christian Religion*, John Calvin
2. *Institutes of the Christian Religion*, John Calvin; *The Death of Death in the Death of Christ*, John Owen; *Knowing God*, J. I. Packer; *The Existence and Attributes of God*, Stephen Charnock; *Chosen by God*, R. C. Sproul
3. Michael Horton (with Rod Rosenbladt and Kim Riddlebarger), James Montgomery Boice, R. C. Sproul
4. *The Death of Death in the Death of Christ*, John Owen

Michael Leach

1. *Ephesians: An Expositional Commentary*, James Montgomery Boice
2. *Systematic Theology*, Louis Berkhof; J. I. Packer's introduction to *The Death of Death in the Death of Christ*, John Owen; *Chosen by God*, R. C. Sproul; *Biblical Theology*, Geerhardus Vos; The Westminster Confession of Faith
3. Sinclair Ferguson, J. Ligon Duncan, R. C. Sproul
4. *Hebrews*, New Testament Commentary series, Simon J. Kistemaker

Lance Lewis

1. *God's Ultimate Purpose*, D. Martyn Lloyd-Jones
2. *Knowing God*, J. I. Packer; *Free at Last?* Carl F. Ellis; *Chosen by God*, R. C. Sproul; *The Reformed Doctrine of Predestination*, Loraine Boettner; *No Place for Truth or Whatever Happened to Evangelical Theology?* David F. Wells
3. James Montgomery Boice, D. Martyn Lloyd-Jones, R. C. Sproul
4. *On Being Black and Reformed*, Anthony Carter

Louis C. Love Jr.

1. *Back to Basics*, ed. David G. Hagopian
2. *God's Passion for His Glory*, John Piper; *The Doctrines of Grace*, James Montgomery Boice and Philip Graham Ryken; *The Biography of D. Martyn Lloyd-Jones*, Iain H. Murray; *The Legacy of Sovereign Joy*, John Piper; *Redemption Accomplished and Applied*, John Murray
3. Robert Crockett Jr., Sherard Burns, Anthony Carter
4. *The Doctrines of Grace*, James Montgomery Boice and Philip Graham Ryken

Eric C. Redmond

1. *The Gospel According to Jesus*, John MacArthur
2. *The Difficult Doctrine of the Love of God*, D. A. Carson; *The Gospel According to Jesus*, John MacArthur; *Redemption Accomplished and Applied*, John Murray; *Desiring God*, John Piper; *The Pleasures of God*, John Piper
3. John Piper, R. C. Sproul, John MacArthur
4. *The Doctrines of Grace*, James Montgomery Boice and Philip Graham Ryken

Roger Skepple

1. *Institutes of the Christian Religion*, John Calvin
2. *Institutes of the Christian Religion*, John Calvin; *Outlines of Theology*, A. A. Hodge; *Systematic Theology*, Charles Hodge; *Dogmatic Theology*, William G. T. Shedd; *Christian's Great Interest*, William Guthrie
3. Paul Fink, Fredrick Howe, John Hannah
4. *Outlines of Theology*, A. A. Hodge

Books Mentioned More Than Once

Knowing God, J. I. Packer (7)
Institutes of the Christian Religion, John Calvin (6)
Systematic Theology, Louis Berkhof (4)
Chosen by God, R. C. Sproul (3)
The Death of Death in the Death of Christ, John Owen (3)
Doctrines of Grace, James Montgomery Boice and Philip Graham Ryken (3)
The Reformed Doctrine of Predestination, Lorraine Boettner (3)
D. Martyn Lloyd-Jones, Iain Murray (2)
Redemption Accomplished and Applied, John Murray (2)

Influential Men Mentioned More Than Once

R. C. Sproul (6)
D. Martyn Lloyd-Jones (2)
James Montgomery Boice (2)
John MacArthur (2)

Notes

Chapter 1: A Plea for Real Answers

1. I have no doubt that this is a more common phenomenon confronting the church's teens than many would care to admit. As common as it is, it could be pleasantly ameliorated by churches' providing solid, straightforward answers to its youths. Why should the church alone insist on dumbing things down? It certainly isn't the tact the schools and universities take!

2. The Bible provides a profound description of this reality: "You were dead in the trespasses and sins in which you once walked, following the course of this world, following the prince of the power of the air, the spirit that is now at work in the sons of disobedience—among whom we all once lived in the passions of the flesh, carrying out the desires of the body and the mind, and were by nature the children of wrath, like the rest of mankind" (Eph. 2:1–3).

3. This phenomenon is also graphically depicted in biblical terms: "And even if our gospel is veiled, it is veiled to those who are perishing. In their case the god of this world has blinded the minds of the unbelievers, to keep them from seeing the light of the gospel of the glory of Christ, who is the image of God. . . . For God, who said, 'Let light shine out of darkness,' has shone in our hearts to give the light of the knowledge of the glory of God in the face of Jesus Christ" (2 Cor. 4:3–6).

4. Ephesians 1:3–5.

5. This is indeed a biblical aspiration, one that should be shared by all believers. "In your hearts honor Christ the Lord as holy, always being prepared to make a defense to anyone who asks you for a reason for the hope that is in you . . ." (1 Pet. 3:15).

6. By historic Christian teachings I mainly mean the teachings of the Protestant Reformation, which to me represents a rediscovery, recovery, and development of the teachings of the apostolic church.

7. While I certainly do not mean to give the impression that there are no "faithful shepherds" in my own African-American context—for that would not be true—I believe there are too many wolves in sheep's clothing roaming through flocks unchecked and uncensored. This is almost the norm among the "big-named," nationally known preachers. These men wield incredible influence among African-American Christians, and they adhere to almost no basic tenets of historical Christianity.

8. While I'm not unmindful that human authors factor in the writing of Scripture, priority still must be given to the divine author: "For no prophecy was ever produced by the will of man, but men spoke from God as they were carried along by the Holy Spirit" (2 Pet. 1:21).

9. TULIP is an acronym that summarizes the final response of the church to questions about John Calvin's teachings that late sixteenth-century Dutch Reformer Jacob Arminius raised. Each letter in TULIP represents a major doctrine of the Scriptures. "T" stands for *total depravity,* the idea that sin so affects humanity that every facet of every person is to some extent tainted by it; "U" is for *unconditional election,* the belief that God singles out whom he wills to receive the gift of eternal life apart from anything they ever did or would do to commend themselves to him. "L" is for *limited atonement,* the conviction that the death of Christ was specifically intended to atone for the sins of those whom God unconditionally elected to save. "I" is for *irresistible grace,* which holds that while God's grace can be opposed, it cannot finally be resisted, and thus never fails to bring those atoned for by Christ's death to faith; and "P" is for *perseverance of the saints,* which is the conviction that everyone elected by God, atoned for by Christ, and brought to faith in Christ will be preserved in that faith till the end.

Chapter 2: From Mecca to the Messiah

1. Then published under the title, *Grace Unknown: The Heart of Reformed Theology.*

Chapter 3: Clemson University Saved My Life

1. The People of the United Methodist Church, http://archives.umc.org/interior.asp?mid=1811.

2. The People of the United Methodist Church, http://www.umc.org/site/c.lwL4KnN1LtH/b.2310047/k.4669/Our_Wesleyan_Theological_Heritage.htm.

3. The Reformed Reader, http://reformedreader.org/t.u.l.i.p.htm.

4. Albert M. Wolters, *Creation Regained: Biblical Basis for a Reformational Worldview* (Grand Rapids, MI: Eerdmans, 2005), 72. http://reformedreader.org/t.u.l.i.p.htm. Emphasis added.

5. Ibid., 78.

6. Ibid., 83.

7. Michael D. Williams, *Far as the Curse Is Found: The Covenant Story of Redemption* (Phillipsburg, NJ: P&R, 2005), 286.

Chapter 4: Doesn't Everyone Believe the Same Thing?

1. Denver Sizemore, *Thirteen Lessons in Christian Doctrine* (Joplin, MO: College Press, 1987, rev. 1997), 98. In summarizing this section on baptism, Sizemore states: "It is clear that salvation comes *after*, not before the act of baptism. It is also clear that baptism alone will not save a person. But the New Testament teaches that when a person truly believes in Christ and genuinely repents of sin, he is then to be baptized into Christ for the remission of his sins," 99.

2. Along with the Reformed confessions and catechisms that grew out of the Reformation, we confess the early creeds of the church, namely the Apostles Creed, the Nicene Creed, and the Athanasius Creed.

3. John Calvin, *Institutes of the Christian Religion*, ed. John T. McNeill, trans. Ford Lewis Battles (Philadelphia: Westminster, 1960): 1:35, 37.

4. Total depravity is the result of Adam's sin. Because of Adam's transgression, sin has passed on to every human being born into this world. This sinfulness is pervasive in that it has touched and affected every aspect of our lives and rendered us helpless in God's sight (Rom. 3:10–11; 8:7–8).

Chapter 6: I Remember It Well

1. A diminutive Englishwoman barely five feet tall, Wendy possessed the enviable characteristics of being warmly engaging, pleasantly challenging, and quietly uncompromising. She freely received the respect of guards and inmates alike, and I have had the speechless pleasure of witnessing both massive male prisoners and rambunctious female inmates shrink away from her by a simple casting of one of her familiar "reassuring" stares. Wendy was deliciously disarming. I credit her for encouraging me to pursue my studies of the Reformed faith.

2. Joel Osteen, *Your Best Life Now: 7 Steps to Living at Your Full Potential* (New York: FaithWords, 2004).

3. Although this terminology has not been specifically used in the historic doctrines of Reformed ecumenism, many of its principles are firmly contained therein. Foremost among its tenets are the total inability of fallen man whom God contemplates as a *massa perditionis*, a mass or crowd of corruption or lost mankind, and man's "absolute exclusion" in the initiation of the saving process so that God's grace and glory may be magnified. See *Benjamin B. Warfield Collection 5*, "Calvin and Calvinism" (Rio, WI: Ages Digital Library, Christian Library Series, 2006), 189. Since the sinner has no intrinsic merit where God is concerned, it is God who freely saves man by his own sovereign design: God savingly loves the sinner for no other reason than he decides to love him; God loves him because God loves him. This is the essence of the divine tautology.

4. L. Russ Bush, *A Handbook for Christian Philosophy* (Grand Rapids, MI: Zondervan, 1991), 312.

5. Other Deuteronomic passages demonstrating the free, divine sovereign election of Israel above all the nations of the earth, all of which belong to God,

through no merit or worth of Israel, are also shown in 9:4–6; 10:14–15; and 14:1–2. See also Amos 3:2. However, none of these resonates with such tautological force and firmness vis-à-vis human demerit as the above verses.

6. Warfield, *Calvin and Calvinism*, 189–90.

7. Willem VanGemeren, *The Promise of Redemption: The Story of Salvation from Creation to the New Jerusalem* (Grand Rapids, MI: Zondervan, 1988), 147–48.

8. Puritan pastor and commentator Matthew Henry expounds, "God fetched the reason of it [i.e., his election] purely from himself." See *Matthew Henry's Commentary*, BibleWorks, version 7.0.019b.3.

9. Warfield, *Calvin and Calvinism*, 188–89.

Chapter 9: Sovereign in a Sweet Home, School, and Solace

1. "HBCU" stands for Historically Black Colleges and Universities.

2. John MacArthur, *The Gospel According to Jesus: What Does Jesus Mean When He Says, "Follow Me"?* (Grand Rapids, MI: Zondervan, 1988). A revised and expanded edition of the book was published in 1994. A second revised edition was published with a new chapter for the twentieth anniversary edition in 2008.

3. MacArthur, *Gospel According to Jesus*, 33.

4. Prior to studying Reformed theology, I recognized a remnant at my home church that was full of love for Christ and obedience to him. The concern expressed in this paragraph has to do with (1) the size of the Sunday attendance and stated membership in comparison to the number of people who actively participated in the process of making disciples of Christ and (2) the lack of accountability for individual growth in Christ. I owe a great debt of love to the people of First Baptist Church of Highland Park for nurturing me in the faith, giving me opportunities to serve, and helping me through seminary.

5. Crisis of *understanding* should not be confused with a crisis of *faith*. I was not losing my faith in Christ. I was only concerned about ordering the faith of which I was certain.

6. Rom. 9:5; 1 Tim. 1:11; cf. Ps. 51:13.

7. Ps. 34:8; 37:4.

8. Eph. 5:25–27.

9. James 1:2–3.

10. Question 1 and Answer 1 of the Westminster Shorter Catechism. Piper introduces Christian hedonism by changing one word: "The chief end of man is to glorify God *by* enjoying him forever," John Piper, *Desiring God: Meditations of a Christian Hedonist* (Sisters, OR: Multnomah, 1986), 13–14, emphasis added.

11. John Piper, *The Pleasures of God: Meditations on God's Delight in Being God* (Sisters, OR: Multnomah, 1991).

12. Piper, *Pleasures of God*, 161–84.

13. Ibid., 48, 192.

14. Piper was the first author I read who emphasized that "God is a mountain spring not a watering trough" (ibid., 241), and that "the Gospel is the

good news that God is the all-satisfying end of all our longings, and that, even though he does not need us, and is in fact estranged from us because of our God-belittling sins, he has, in the great love with which he has loved us, made a way for sinners to drink at the river of his delights through Jesus Christ" (ibid., 203). He writes, "A mountain spring is self-replenishing. It constantly overflows and supplies others. But a watering trough needs to be filled with a pump or bucket brigade. So if you want to glorify the worth of a watering trough you work hard to keep it full and useful. But if you want to glorify the worth of a spring you do it by getting down on your hands and knees and drinking to your heart's satisfaction, until you have the refreshment and strength to go back down the valley and tell people what you've found. You do not glorify a mountain spring by dutifully hauling water up the path from the river below and dumping it in the spring. What we have seen is that God is like a mountain spring, not a watering trough. And since that is the way God is, we are not surprised to learn from Scripture—and our faith is strengthened to hold fast—that the way to please God is to come to him to get and not to give, to drink and not to water. He is most glorified in us when we are most satisfied in him. My hope as a desperate sinner, who lives in a Death Valley desert of unrighteousness, hangs on this biblical truth: that God is the kind of God who will be pleased with the one thing I have to offer—my thirst. That is why the sovereign freedom and self-sufficiency of God are so precious to me: they are the foundation of my hope that God is delighted not by the resourcefulness of bucket brigades, but by the bending down of broken sinners to drink at the fountain of grace" (ibid., 215–16).

15. I encourage readers to see the research of Keith Augustus Burton, *The Blessing of Africa: The Bible and African Christianity* (Downers Grove, IL: InterVarsity, 2007); Elizabeth Isichei, *A History of Christianity in Africa: From Antiquity to the Present* (Grand Rapids, MI: Eerdmans, 1995); Thomas C. Oden, *How Africa Shaped the Christian Mind: Rediscovering the Seedbed of Western Christianity* (Downers Grove, IL: InterVarsity, 2007); Mark Shaw, *The Kingdom of God in Africa: A Short History of African Christianity* (Grand Rapids, MI: Baker, 1997).

16. John Sailant, *Black Puritan, Black Republican: The Life and Thought of Lemuel Haynes, 1753–1833* (New York: Oxford, 2002).

17. W. E. B. Dubois, *The Souls of Black Folk* (New York: Signet, 1982).

18. Eric C. Redmond, "Review of *On Being Black and Reformed: A New Perspective on the African-American Christian Experience*," *Journal of African-American Southern Baptist History* 2 (June 2004): 102–8.

19. By erecting two logical syllogisms to reflect this reasoning, I can demonstrate the logical fallacies:

	Syllogism 1	Syllogism 2
Major Premises:	God decreed Antebellum slavery	Antebellum slavery was unjust
Minor Premises:	Antebellum slavery was unjust	God cannot be unjust
Conclusions:	God is unjust	God could not have decreed Antebellum slavery

The first syllogism does not consider the human factors in Antebellum slavery. For, logically speaking, God could have easily decreed a just form of Antebellum slavery akin to indentured servitude. But entire governments, many slave owners, and slave traders maintained a system of injustice. Therefore, it is not logically valid to conclude God is unjust from the premises. Moreover, one has every assurance from Scripture that God is just (Gen. 18:25; Deut. 32:4; Ps. 7:9, 11; 67:4; 96:10, 13; 99:4; 116:5; Isa. 5:16; 11:4; 41:10; 45:21; Dan. 9:14; Acts 17:31; Rom. 3:21–26; 2 Thess. 1:5; Heb. 6:10; 1 Pet. 3:18), and that his justice is completely dependent upon his absolute rule over all things (i.e., he is the Judge "of *all* the earth" [Gen. 18:25], he will judge "*every* deed . . . *every* secret thing" [Eccl. 12:14] and "*every* careless word" [Matt. 12:36], "he will judge the *world* in righteousness" [Acts 17:31], "*no* creature is hidden from his sight . . . to whom we must give account" [Heb. 4:13], and "*every* knee shall bow" to him [Isa. 45:23; Rom. 14:11; Phil. 2:10–11]).

In the second syllogism, the conclusion is not reasoned from the premises because the premises do not concern God's decree. The only thing that can be concluded from this syllogism is that God did not cause the injustice of Antebellum slavery. Humanly speaking this leaves us with a paradox, but not a contradiction. God has decreed all things, and God is completely just. Both are true. We see evidence of both truths in God's great love for us in killing his own Son (Acts 4:10; Isa. 53:10).

The injustice of Antebellum slavery does not disintegrate the sovereign decree of God. Instead, we are left with mystery about the working of a holy God as we affirm both his goodness and his eternal rule. More significantly, we would be left with a terrible dilemma if God had no control of the Middle Passage and the Antebellum period. We would need to wonder why he was not in control, if it was a matter of power or goodness. Again, Reformed theology, by preaching the sovereign God of the Scriptures, avoids such a theological dilemma.

20. I have been helped in my understanding of Reformed theology by reading primary sources. Such reading has warded off some of the caricatures of Reformed theology I have heard, such as "Calvin was not even a Calvinist"— meaning that he did not believe in election—that "Spurgeon was not a Calvinist," and the general (false) idea that Reformed theology exclusively limits the work of the atonement to the elect. However, John Calvin believed in election, the limited efficacy of the atonement, while yet acknowledging a general effect of the atonement on all people, as expressed in the following quotes:

> He makes this favour common to all, because it is propounded to all, and not because it is in reality extended to all; for though Christ suffered for the sins of the whole world, and is offered through God's benignity indiscriminately to all, yet all do not receive him (John Calvin, *Calvin's Commentaries: Romans–Galatians* [Wilmington, DE: Associated, 1971], 1401; comments on Rom. 5:18).

> It is hence evident, how foolishly some maintain, that all are indiscriminately the elect, because the doctrine of salvation is universal, and because God invites all indiscriminately to himself. But the generality of the promises do not alone and by itself make salvation common to all: on the contrary, the particular revelation,

mentioned by the Prophet, confines it to the elect (Calvin, *Calvin's Commentaries: Romans–Galatians*, 1470; comments on Rom. 10:16).

It is a remarkable commendation of faith, that it frees us from everlasting destruction. For he intended expressly to state that, though we appear to have been born to death, undoubted deliverance is offered to us by the faith of Christ; and therefore, that we ought not to fear death, which otherwise hangs over us. And he has employed the universal term *whosoever*, both to invite all indiscriminately to partake of life, and to cut off every excuse from unbelievers. Such is also the import of the term *World*, which he formerly used; for though nothing will be found in *the world* that is worthy of the favour of God, yet he shows himself to be reconciled to the whole world, when he invites all men without exception to the faith of Christ, which is nothing else than an entrance to life.

Let us remember, on the other hand, that while *life* is promised universally to *all who believe* in Christ, still faith is not common to all. For Christ is made known and held out to the view of all, but the elect alone are they whose eyes God opens, that they may seek him by faith. Here, too, is displayed a wonderful effect of faith; for by it we receive Christ such as he is given to us by the Father—that is, as having freed us from the condemnation of eternal death, and made us heirs of eternal life, because, by the sacrifice of his death, he has atoned for our sins, that nothing may prevent God from acknowledging us as his sons. Since, therefore, faith embraces Christ, with the efficacy of his death and the fruit of his resurrection, we need not wonder if by it we obtain likewise the life of Christ (John Calvin, *Commentary on the Holy Gospel of Jesus Christ according to John*, Calvin's Commentaries [Grand Rapids, MI: Baker, 1981]: 16:124–125; comments on John 3:16).

But how can such an imprecation be reconciled with the mildness of an apostle, who ought to wish that all should be saved, and that not a single person should perish? So far as men are concerned, I admit the force of this argument; for it is the will of God that we should seek the salvation of all men without exception, as Christ suffered for the sins of the whole world. But devout minds are sometimes carried beyond the consideration of men, and led to fix their eye on the glory of God, and the kingdom of Christ. The glory of God, which is in itself more excellent than the salvation of men, ought to receive from us a higher degree of esteem and regard. Believers earnestly desirous that the glory of God should be promoted, forget men, and forget the world, and would rather choose that the whole world should perish, than that the smallest portion of the glory of God should be withdrawn (John Calvin, *Commentaries on the Epistles of Paul to the Galatians and Ephesians*, Calvin's Commentaries [Grand Rapids: Baker, 1981]: 21:157; comments on Gal. 5:12).

Similarly, Spurgeon expressed his firm belief in the definite atoning work of Christ while leaving room for the mysterious working of God in the atonement for the non-elect:

God might doubtless have acted upon another plan, and have given Christ power only over his elect if he had willed, that he might give eternal life to them; but it has not so pleased God. It has, on the contrary, pleased him to put the whole race under the mediatorial sway of Jesus, in order that he might give eternal life to those who were chosen out of the world. God might have commissioned his servants to go into the world and preach the gospel to the chosen: he might have told us to present Christ only to certain persons upon whom there should be a peculiar mark; it has not so pleased him; he bids us go "into all the world, and preach the gospel to every creature," his high decree and divine intent being that those whom he hath ordained unto eternal life shall, through believing, enter into the life which he hath ordained for them. I do not know whether I have brought before you what I am certain is the full idea of the text—a general power given to the Mediator over all flesh, as the result of which a proclamation of mercy is universally published to men, and a general declaration of salvation through faith presented to all creatures, but this always with a special, limited, definite design, that a chosen people, separated from before all worlds from the rest of mankind should obtain eternal life. I have aimed in my ministry constantly to preach, as far as I can, the whole of the gospel rather than a fragment of it. Hence, those brethren who are sounder than the Bible abhor me as much as if I were an Arminian; and on the other side, the enemies of the doctrine of grace often represent me as an Ultra-Calvinist. I am rejoined to receive the censure of both sides; I am not ambitious to be numbered in the master roll of either party. I have never cultivated the acquaintance nor desired the approbation of those men who shut their eyes to the truths which they do not wish to see. I never desired to be reputed so excessively Calvinistic as to neglect one part of Scripture in order to maintain another. If I am thought to be inconsistent with myself, I am very glad to be so, so long as I am not inconsistent with Holy Scripture. Sure I am that all truth is *really* consistent, but equally certain am I that it is not *apparently* so to our poor, finite minds. In nine cases out of ten, he who is nervously anxious to be manifestly consistent with himself in his theological system, if he gains his end, is merely consistent with a fool; he who is consistent with Scripture is consistent with perfect wisdom; he who is consistent with himself is at best consistent with imperfection, folly, and insignificance. To keep to Scripture, even though it should involve a charge of personal inconsistency, is to be faithful to God and men's souls. My text seems to me to present that double aspect which so many people either cannot or will not see. Here is the great atonement by which the Mediator has the whole world put under his dominion; but still here is a special object for this atonement, the ingathering, or rather outgathering of a chosen and peculiar people unto eternal life (C. H. Spurgeon, "General and Yet Particular," *The Metropolitan Tabernacle Pulpit* [Pasadena, TX: Pilgrim, reprint 1976], 10:230–231; Sermon on John 17:2, April 24, 1864).

Both Calvin and Spurgeon held, preached, and taught Reformed theology, and their teaching allowed room for the mysterious working of the sovereign God. The same could be said of the modern New Testament scholar D. A. Carson's teaching on Reformed theology when he writes,

When he says he loves us, does not God rather mean something like the following? "Morally speaking, you are the people of the halitosis, the bulbous nose, the greasy hair, the disjointed knees, the abominable personality. Your sins have made you disgustingly ugly. But I love you anyway, not because you are attractive, but because it is my nature to love." And in the case of the elect, God adds, "I have set my affection on you from before the foundation of the universe, not because you are wiser or better or stronger than others but because in grace I chose to love you. You are mine, and you will be transformed. Nothing in all creation can separate you from my love mediated through Jesus Christ" (Rom. 8) (D. A. Carson, *The Difficult Doctrine of the Love of God* [Wheaton, IL: Crossway, 2000], 63).

21. Lev. 19:35–37; Prov. 16:11; 20:23; James 2:1–13; 5:1–6.
22. Eph. 4:28.
23. Rom. 12:10; Gal. 6:1–5.
24. Luke 3:14; 2 Cor. 9:8; 12:10; 1 Tim. 6:6–10; Heb. 13:5.
25. Phil. 4:10–12.
26. 1 Pet. 2:13–25.
27. Matt. 6:19–34.

Chapter 10: Looking for Love in All the Wrong Places
1. John MacArthur, *The Vanishing Conscience* (Dallas: Word, 1994), 128.

Index

Index